What Church Members Wish *Ministers* Knew

What Church Members Wish *Ministers* Knew

Jan G. Linn

Chalice Press
St. Louis, Missouri

Scripture quotations not otherwise designated are from the *New Revised Standard Version Bible,* copyright 1989, Division of Christian Education of the National Council of Churches of Christ in the United States of America and are used by permission.

Scripture quotations marked RSV are from the *Revised Standard Version* of the Bible, copyrighted 1946, 1952, © 1971, 1973.

Cover illustration/design: Doug Hall
Art Director: Michael Domínguez

2 3 4 5 6 7 8 9 10   99 98 97

Library of Congress Cataloging-in-Publication Data

What church members wish ministers knew/Jan G. Linn.
    p.   cm.
    ISBN 0-8272-4234-4
    1. Clergy—Office. 2. Pastoral theology. 3. Laity. 4. Church membership. I. Title.
BV660.2.L55   1995
253—dc20   95-34009
                                                  CIP

Printed in the United States of America

For
Lucille Ferrell

Acknowledgments

Writing is never work done in a vacuum. A finished book reflects influences that are conscious and unconscious, direct and indirect, solicited and happenstance. Thus, expressing appreciation to all the people who helped to make this book better than it would have been is not possible. Yet there are specific individuals and groups to whom a public expression of gratitude is both appropriate and necessary.

To the congregation of Harrodsburg Christian Church, Harrodsburg, Kentucky, and to the pastor and personal friend, David Hartman, I am deeply grateful for inviting me to speak to the topic of things church members wish ministers knew. It was one of those truly joyous occasions in ministry not soon to be forgotten.

To Lexington Theological Seminary, its students, staff and faculty, who make this a special place, I express sincere appreciation for the hours of conversations and discussions that helped to shape the content of this material, and for the personal privilege it is to serve in ministry in such a community.

To Michael Kinnamon, academic dean, colleague, and trusted friend, I am truly indebted for his affirmation and support of the ministry of writing in general, and for specific suggestions for this material regarding the social conscience and ecumenical impulses that are alive and well among the laity.

To Joy, who read the material at every point along the way, and whose many suggestions helped bring clarity of thought and expression, I am more than grateful. I am overflowing with love as we share life together in our home and in the ministry of the church.

Finally to Lucille Ferrell, the best church member I know, who read the material twice, regularly encouraged me—even "pushed" a bit—to speak candidly about issues of concern to church members, and who noted the "clergy" tone of the material in more than a few places, I owe much gratitude. Every church deserves a Lucille Ferrell as a member, and every minister needs one. It is to this loved one whose entire life has been a witness of faith and faithfulness that this book is dedicated.

Contents

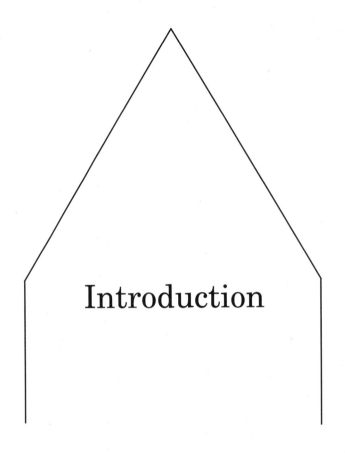

Introduction

This is not a book I ever anticipated writing. When *What Ministers Wish Church Members Knew* was first published, more than a few laypeople said they wanted to write a sequel about what church members wish ministers knew. My response each time was that I would be glad to read it if they ever wrote it. And I meant it. Without question there are many things ministers need to know, things many church members probably do wish the minister of their particular congregation knew. Even more, a book about such things could continue the dialogue on ministry issues between ministers and church members that the publication of *What Ministers Wish...* got started. It's just that I did not think seriously about writing such a book myself.

1

Then I awakened one morning to an avalanche of ideas for just such a book. Within a relatively brief period of time the chapter titles made their way onto the screen of my computer. The book in your hand is the result.

Yet the basic question remained unsettled in my mind. Was I the one to write a book about what church members wish ministers knew? Ordained ministry is my vocation. This fact has more than a modest influence on my thinking. I think about church and ministry not only as a church member, but as one who is called clergy. A book of this nature would be written from that particular perspective. Acknowledging that I could not speak for laypeople, could I as an ordained minister at least speak on their behalf?

In reflecting upon the ease with which the chapter titles had unexpectedly come to mind, it occurred to me that in the course of leading retreats and workshops in numerous churches for several years, I had listened carefully to what church members were saying about ministers in general, and their minister in particular. It was possible that the chapter titles came so easily precisely because they reflected the things I had heard laity saying. While the responsibility for the content of each chapter is solely mine, what is written here attempts to express the thoughts and feelings of a broad spectrum of church members who support, work with, and pray for the ordained ministers in their congregations and parishes. Though the words are mine, I want to believe the book belongs to them.

While this book and *What Ministers Wish...* stand on their own, the material in this volume needs to be read within the context of both. *What Ministers Wish...* sought to speak to the laity on behalf of the ordained clergy. *What Church Members Wish...* intends the reverse, to speak to clergy on behalf of the laity. At the same time, though, this is not to suggest that this book, or any book, can speak for all church members. If anything, the following chapters constitute a challenge to the notion that ministers can speak with authority in saying, "Church members believe…" or, "Church members think…." No such claims can be made. For this reason every effort has been made to avoid making sweeping generalizations about Christian laity.

In *What Ministers Wish…* every effort was made not to be overly critical of laity. A similar concern for my colleagues in ministry has guided this work. Yet this book has a different tone than that of *What Ministers Wish….* Readers of both volumes will find a somewhat less "playful" mood in this material. In all honesty I am not sure why this is the case. Most likely it reflects the fact that I am an ordained minister as well as a church member. It is possible that the difference in the tone of the two books is more a matter of emphasis than substance. Or perhaps the difference simply reflects the difference in my own mood at the time of the writing of each.

What I do know is that writing this book has been an exciting challenge. Trying to speak to ministerial colleagues about the concerns and expectations of the church members with whom they serve invited both candor and compassion. The intention has been to be pastoral and provocative. The challenge itself has proven to be a source of power and energy to complete the task. Writing is ministry for me. I have found that little else compares to the excitement of believing that what one is writing may be important and timely.

In a deep sense writing this book has been a labor of love and hope. It is written for all who love the church and pray for its life and witness. The church is as strong or weak as those of us who are its flesh and bones. It is my hope that this book, and *What Ministers Wish…*, can excite church members and ministers to renewed vision, commitment, and joy about church life today.

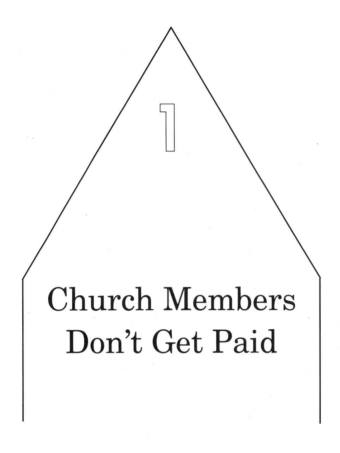

Church Members
Don't Get Paid

Sometimes the most obvious things in life are the ones most overlooked or taken for granted. One is the fact that the church is a community of volunteers. This reality forms the character of the church as the body of Christ. Whatever else church members are, the one thing they have always been and probably always will be is a volunteer participant in the church. How could any minister forget this? Well, most likely most ministers don't. More likely is the fact that more than a few ministers take the voluntary nature of church life for granted.

It is true, of course, that church membership means belonging to the mystical body of Christ, which is no small thing. Church membership is the tangible expression of union with Jesus Christ. That carries the expectation that a church member will seek to follow the will of Jesus to love God and to love neighbor. Most of us have heard ministers speak often and at length about the responsibilities of this duality of loving that accompanies membership in the church.

For more than a few years of church history church membership was defined primarily in terms of being a good citizen. This meant that the focus of one's energies as a Christian was outside rather than inside the church. Communicants attended mass or worship in order to be moral and ethical during the routine of daily life. The internal affairs of the church were left in the hands of priests.

It was not until after the sixteenth-century Protestant Reformation that this view of church membership began to change. The growth of Protestant denominations— another issue in itself—saw a commensurate rise in institutional programs and ministries. The truth of the matter is that money and people were needed to support this growth of activity. Here in North America congregational life became the focus of church life, and every congregation was dependent as much on church members as ordained clergy to do the work of ministry and to pay for it. Today the average congregation— mainline, oldline, or sideline—depends primarily on the support and involvement of church members to keep going.

In an ideal world the fact that church members do not get paid to be at church or to be involved in church would make no difference in terms of their commitment to service. Being a Christian would be motivation enough. But the world we live in is hardly ideal, and the truth is, for the majority of church members, the church is simply one place among many to spend their time and energy, not to mention their money. Churches in any city or community, small or large, compete for the attention and commitment of their members with a variety of community service groups and organizations, from the Red Cross to the school board to the Scouts to Little League.

To a larger degree than many ministers would admit, these other groups are worthy ways for people to spend their time. Parents show loving support and encouragement to their children by volunteering to coach, be the team driver, and otherwise always attend events their children are involved in. In a time of family breakdown and little time for family togetherness, this is sometimes the primary way parents and children spend time together. It may not be the way things should be. It is the way they are, and ministers have to face this fact.

Add to these demands the fact that in the majority of marriages now both husband and wife work outside the home, and it becomes obvious that the time and energy crunch increases significantly. Most ministers know this to be the case. Yet many ministers—too many, in fact—also find it very difficult to appreciate the time people actually do give to their church.

One of the ways this lack of appreciation shows itself is in the disappointment ministers often feel over the lack of attendance at worship services and/or special meetings and gatherings. As one who is often a guest speaker at such gatherings, I frequently hear the protestations and frustrations of ministers about what they see as a lack of support of and commitment to the church by the members. When disappointment turns into discouragement, ministers will usually make the decision to leave that congregation and seek a new start somewhere else. These ministers lose sight of the many church members who give more than they have a right to expect. They lose sight of what church members like B.B. Holdren give to the church.

B.B. worked on the assembly line at the General Electric plant in his community for more than twenty years, until crippling MS finally forced him to take disability. Every week of those twenty years B.B. worshiped in his church on Sunday, supported through his weekly attendance a coffee house ministry his church sponsored, and met every Monday night in a small group who had the dream of renewing inner city life in his community through a housing ministry for the poor. This group eventually started delivering firewood to the poorest of the poor, and he was always there to help whenever they did. In addition to this kind of voluntary service to his church, B.B. managed to be a husband and father. It was a long-overdue and well-deserved recognition when the local GE plant nominated him for the national service award among all GE workers. He won the award.

B.B. Holdren was a volunteer. He was never paid to do what he did, and never wanted to be. Some of us who worked with him were paid by the church to do ministry. It was what we were expected to do. B.B. did it because he wanted to. His only incentive was the intrinsic value of the ministry itself. It was nothing short of amazing that he would work all day and then give the time and energy he gave, in the face of a gradually deteriorating body, for all those years.

While the B.B. Holdrens of the world may not be legion, their kind live in communities and serve in churches everywhere. Too often ministers let church members who are not the B.B. Holdren type dominate their thinking about what church members are like. Most of us who preach have on at least one occasion, and probably more, preached our disappointment and discouragement to the B.B. Holdrens in our churches who ought to inspire and encourage us. Each time this has happened we have robbed them of hearing the message of hope and joy in the gospel they deserve to hear. These are the very people who need to hear a word of encouragement themselves. They need to know that what they do is special and appreciated.

They don't do what they do for recognition, any more than ministers do what they do for recognition. But no one has ever died from too much appreciation. Faithful church members deserve to be appreciated. They give and give without pay or even recognition. The fact is they do not have to do anything they do. They are not required to be devoted to their church. They could easily sit at home rather than attend a church meeting that all too often is boring and, in some instances, discouraging in itself. They could sleep in and take Sunday morning for needed relaxation and family time. Instead they come to church. They attend dull meetings. They volunteer to serve in soup kitchens and food pantries and church bazaars and search committees for a new minister. These are the saints of the rank and file.

It is an occupational hazard in ministry not to remember that what these people do is voluntary. They don't get paid. Their reward is the intrinsic value of their service. It is no small thing they do being volunteers. Ministers would be well served to remember that.

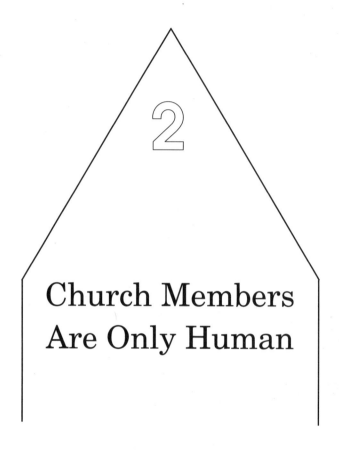

Church Members
Are Only Human

A true story. A couple recently left the church where they had been members for more than thirty years to join one closer to their home. It made sense. Both of them are now retired. And both have been active leaders in the church all their adult lives. They had served in every lay leadership position there was in their previous church home, sometimes the same position more than once. The church did not have any more reliable leaders than these two. When either had a responsibility in the church, no one ever had to worry that something would be forgotten or simply not get done. Nothing would ever stop them from fulfilling their responsibilities. Most of the time they went far beyond the call of duty, doing more than they were asked to do, and always pitching in when someone else needed help.

But this couple have a serious flaw from which they do not seem to be able to escape. They are—well, they are "human." They have feet made of clay. Because they care so much about their church, they are intense about the work they do in it and in its name. They are so human they care about everything that goes on in the church. As you might expect, this means they sometimes, even often, ask questions and have opinions about things in which they have no direct involvement. They believe that whatever goes on in the church concerns them. Sometimes this can be frustrating to others who are in leadership, especially when either of them becomes more intense about an issue than seems justified. As we have said, these people are human, and their humanness, like most of us, shows up all the time.

Their humanness showed up in the congregation they left, and it bothered the minister a lot. He found them to be intrusive and nagging, always sticking their noses where he believed they didn't belong. He was not hesitant in letting them know how he felt. He ignored them as much as possible. They attempted to talk to him to find out why they bothered him so much. They believed they were trying to help him. He thought otherwise.

Perhaps he *and* they were right. In trying to help, that is, with good intentions and motivation, maybe they tried too much and too hard. They finally reached the conclusion that it was time to act on something they had considered for several years—visiting the church to which they now belong to see if they might feel at home and be needed in some way. The minister with whom they were in conflict was not open to discussing their decision to leave, or the tension that had so long existed between them. They left the church quietly and gracefully. Not once did they publicly criticize the minister or try to gather support for themselves in opposition to him. They cared too much about this church they had loved and served for so many years to do that. They just gradually pulled away.

Any minister can sometimes feel like a church member is more of a problem than a help. After all, the ordained of Christ's church are as human as the next person. But what this minister, and all ministers, can so easily forget is that church members are also human. And they will never be anything other than human. They make mistakes. They can be difficult to work with. They can be hardheaded and stubborn and a pain to be around. They can be unkind and even mean-spirited. They can also be wonderful and do wonderful things.

Churches are full of problems, and the reason is actually quite simple. People can't stop being people. Even though the gospel speaks of new birth and transformation, its effect does not enable any of us to get out of our skin. We know this, of course. Yet ministers often talk about and act toward church members as if they don't realize this.

Once, during a period of intense frustration about some members being so upset about the direction I was trying to lead a church, I shared my feelings in a retreat with lay leaders who were supporting what we were trying to do. One of them was a retired personnel director for a major corporation. He listened to what I said and then responded: "Jan, I am surprised that you are so surprised by the response you are getting. Their attitude is so predictable. They are just being human. They don't know how to be anything else."

He went on to explain that he was not justifying their reactions or attitudes or behavior. He was simply pointing out the obvious. Their humanness was showing all over the place in ways that were not helpful. Then he reminded me that all of us were sinners, after all. All of us fall short of the glory of God. No one is perfect.

It is easy for ministers to become cynical about church members. It is not shocking in ministerial circles to hear someone say that one or two funerals of certain church members would surely make things easier at the church. It is not said in seriousness, of course, but the fact that it is said at all, and that no one is shocked by it, reveals a basic cynicism to which more than a few ministers fall prey. It is a cynicism rooted in ministers showing how all too human they are in seeing the specks in the eyes of church members while not seeing the planks in their own. The truth of the matter is that church members have to put up with the human frailties and weakness of ministers every bit as much as ministers have to do so with church members.

This failure to accept the humanness of church members can prevent ministers from recognizing the good that exists in the church. In his little book *Life Together*, a book about Christian community, Dietrich Bonhoeffer warned his students against constantly complaining about their congregations. He told them they should enter the fellowship of the underground seminary community of which they were a part as "thankful recipients." Without this kind of attitude they will "hinder God from letting our fellowship grow according to the measure and riches which are there for us all in Jesus Christ." Finally, he told them: "The more thankfully we daily receive what is given to us, the more surely and steadily will fellowship increase and grow from day to day as God pleases" (pp. 28–30).

What church members wish ministers knew, and would never forget, is that they are nothing more and nothing less than human, doing wonderful and foolish things, helping and getting in the way at the same time. Church members know they can be loving and hateful, that they can be adult and also act like children. They just wish ministers would remember that all of this is rooted in the simple fact of life that church members, like ministers, are people. It's the best and worst any of us can be and do.

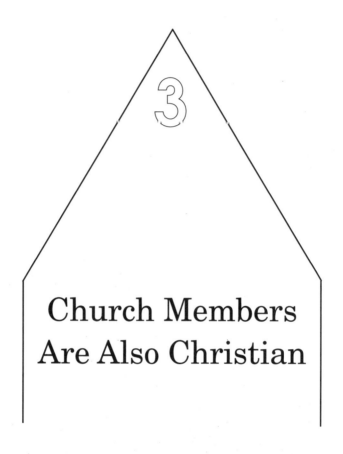

Church Members
Are Also Christian

In spite of the fact that church members, like ministers, are human and, as such, are sinful, the practical effect being that they are sometimes difficult to work with, they are, nonetheless, like ministers, saved by the grace of God in Jesus Christ. This is the good news! Moreover, by virtue of their baptism many church members have taken the next step and claimed being saved by grace as the defining truth for their lives. In doing so they are claiming that they are what being Christian means— they are Christ-ones. They belong to Christ. The sinful nature of their humanness, like ministers, does not alter the reality of their Christ-oneness. Church members are followers of Jesus Christ. Daily they prove, like ministers, that they are human. But nothing changes the fact that they are Christians.

Sometimes just how Christian they are is nothing short of amazing. Laura Santana and her husband, Josh, are notable examples of this point. Laura is an educator for the board of education in her state. Josh is an attorney. Their professional competence has been recognized by their peers and employers. They are successful by all contemporary secular standards. They are people of means and power. Their life is good and full. They enjoy the kind of life many people find enviable.

Yet their professional and social success is not the standard by which they define themselves. Rather, the defining reality in their lives is their commitment to Jesus Christ. Josh and Laura Santana are Christians. They take their church membership seriously. They have shown this in the primary responsibility they have taken in the last two years for the stewardship program of their large, historic church. Unsatisfied with the traditional view of stewardship as a program of financial pledges to undergird the annual budget, Laura and Josh have spent hours studying and planning a comprehensive stewardship educational program for their church. Their reason for doing this has been, by their own admission, because they have needed more of a challenge than simply giving money to support their church. They want to know how to live as better stewards in God's world.

What a gift they are to their church! Their level of commitment to living as Christians against great odds is inspiring. It would be easy, if not tempting, for them to be nominal church members, trying to be good people, but absorbed by a busy schedule of a basically secular life. They could have played the voluntary nature of church membership to their own advantage, taking a "don't call me, I'll call you" attitude about their involvement. But they have chosen a different path for themselves. One might even describe it as a straight and narrow one that many people never find.

What Laura and Josh believe is that church member-ship is discipleship. The spirit of their volunteerism in their church is expressed by the word *vocation*, derived from the Latin *vocare*, which means "calling." For the Santanas, theirs is a "holy" calling. They seek the rule of God in their lives on a daily basis. They do not want to become ordained. They love their professional work. Be-ing members of the laity is enough for them. They do what they do intentionally solely because being church members means living as Christians to the extent that they understand how to do so.

Ministers with any sense covet members like Laura and Josh Santana in their congregations. Yet many min-isters have the attitude that most church members have settled for nominal membership, and that the minister is the only person in the congregation who takes the faith seriously. It is not uncommon to find in ministers deep levels of hostility toward church members. Apparently the humanness of church members about which we have already written has overwhelmed these ministers, lead-ing them to doubt the sincerity of commitment of most of the people with whom they work. They may find a Laura and Josh Santana once in a while, but for the most part, many ministers believe they are throwing pearls among swine.

The temptation to cynicism is a force to be reckoned with in most ministers. Church members can spot a cyni-cal minister at thirty paces. What ministers need to un-derstand is that confronting this temptation involves more than trying to avoid becoming cynical. The issue is funda-mentally theological. What is at stake here is whether ministers can trust the power and work of the Holy Spirit to blow where it will and reap a harvest in places unex-pected, often coming as a surprise. Who can know with certainty that a church member is not sincerely commit-ted to the gospel? Who can get into the mind and heart of another to know the purity of his or her soul? Indeed, what if the level of commitment among church members is due at least in part to the failure of ministers to teach the demands and joys of taking the yoke of Christ upon oneself? Perhaps the work of the Spirit has gone only as deep as ministers have led their church members to go.

In *Life Together*, Bonhoeffer was concerned that his students, in their idealism about the nature of the church, might be quick to judge Christian community by the standard of individual piety and spirituality. He cautioned them that neither of these constitutes Christian community; rather, it is what we are by reason of Christ that forms the basis of community. Unless they understood this, he wrote, they would be susceptible and even overwhelmed by "a great disillusionment with others, with Christians in general" (p. 27).

Bonhoeffer then became more pointed, writing:

Only God knows the real state of our fellowship, of our sanctification. What may appear weak and trifling to us may be great and glorious to God. Just as the Christian should not be constantly feeling his spiritual pulse, so, too, the Christian Community has not been given to us by God for us to be constantly taking its temperature.

He continued:

Christian brotherhood [community] is not an ideal which we must realize; it is, rather a reality created by God in Christ in which we participate (p. 30).

The spiritual issue at stake here is what in scripture is dealt with in the context of passing judgment upon one another. In the Sermon on the Mount Jesus makes it quite clear that judging another person is risky business, for, he says, "with the judgment you make you will be judged" (Matthew 7:2). He goes on to suggest that those tempted to see the faults of others would be better served tending to their own (7:3). In John's Gospel we find this same sentiment painted in graphic colors in the story of the woman caught in adultery (8:3–11). Jesus is not only saying that we should not judge others. He is saying that we cannot judge another with integrity, if we are self-conscious at all about the humanness from which none of us can escape, as discussed in chapter 2.

In general, most ministers do not think that they make these kinds of judgments on church members. At the same time there are hardly any of us in ordained ministry who have not been found wondering at least to ourselves on occasion whether we are serving people who are really Christian.

Well, they are! And they know when ministers think they aren't. Ministers need to remember that the words of Jesus teach that no cause and no person is served by a judgmental attitude. Life sometimes requires judgment on transitory issues. The cause of weighty matters, on the other hand, is hurt rather than advanced by an attitude that is quick to judge and slow to listen.

Novelist Barbara Kingsolver makes this very point in a marvelous novel entitled *Animal Dreams*. At one point the book's main character, Cosima Noline, tries to get an apathetic high school science class to start taking the destruction of the environment seriously in an impassioned speech just before the class day ends. As soon as the students start leaving, Cosima begins to regret the humiliating way she used one of the male students who was wearing stone-washed jeans to illustrate her argument. Companies wash these jeans in a special kind of gravel dug out of the volcanic mountains of the Southwest to give them their worn look. The digging ends up destroying the mountain sides in the process. The young man's girlfriend stayed after class to talk to Cosima. She told her that she noticed that Cosima sometimes wears the same kind of jeans, to which Cosima replies, "I've been learning a lot about this stuff just lately. I'm not saying I'm not part of the problem." The young woman then asked, "So how come you're so mad at us?" Cosima is embarrassed. She replies, "Connie, I don't really know. Because I'm guilty, too, I guess. And now I'm trying to fix it all at once."

There are times when ministers make the same mistake, and church members think we are mad at them, blaming them alone for the condition of the church and the world, implying that they may be church members but they surely aren't Christians. As churches deal with sensitive and complex issues unyielding to simple solutions, all congregations would be strengthened if ministers thought and acted from the conviction that their church members really are Christians. Church members need this kind of affirmation. Church members, like ministers, are part of the problems we face in the church and in the world. That does not change the fact that they are also Christians.

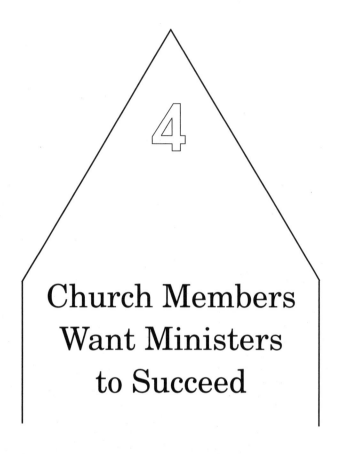

Church Members
Want Ministers
to Succeed

Church members want ministers to succeed. Not all
ministers have heard this news, but it's true—which
means church members on the whole want the relationship between the minister and church members to be
good. Not only do church members want ministers to
succeed; many pray daily for them. This is something
ministers can easily take for granted. What a marvelous
gift ministers have in knowing that church members are
praying for them daily because of the role they play in
members lives!

Serving on a ministerial search committee is a task
not to be taken lightly. It is among the most important
responsibilities any church member can be involved in.
Anyone who has served in this capacity knows how de-

manding this work can be. When a search committee recommends a minister to be called by the congregation, every member is saying this is someone they believe in and want to succeed in ministry with their church. When the congregation votes to extend the call, everyone who votes in the positive is saying the same thing. Even in churches where ministers are appointed, they are received by congregations in the hope and with the prayer that they will succeed. Almost without exception ministries begin in the firm expectation that they will succeed.

Sometimes tensions in ministry can cloud the fact that church members really do want ministers to succeed. This is not to say that there are no church members who don't try to undermine ministry. Some do, and sometimes they succeed. But this fact should not lead to the conclusion that most church members are this way. They are not. Ministers enjoy much goodwill from their members. Many times church members are more tolerant and understanding of their minister than they experience themselves in their own workplaces. The ministers who do not realize this often read the signs wrong and end up drawing unproductive lines between themselves and their church members.

It is sad to see this kind of thing happen. A minister went to a church that everyone knew was anxious for a good ministry. That is why he was encouraged by several different people outside the church to accept the call. After a year there this young man began to talk with colleagues about the opposition he was facing in his ministry. Only a few years of experience in ministry were necessary to see right away that he was reading the signs wrong, that what he was interpreting as opposition to him was simply local tradition that seemed intractable. Those colleagues close to the church told him that they had heard only positive comments about how things were going. But here he was ready to quit.

It is not easy to remember—and believe—that church members really do want their minister to succeed. Resistance to change is such a common experience in the church that a minister can misread what is happening in a ministry as a whole. But the primary point is the *intentions* of church members. In one sense quality ministry depends upon the goodwill of church members toward ministers. In reality, however, it is the *trust* ministers have in this goodwill that finally makes the difference. As we have already said, it is easy for ministers to miss the goodwill that is prevalent among the vast majority of their members. The value and gift of this goodwill are diminished considerably if ministers don't believe the goodwill is there. It is also possible that trusting in this goodwill helps to make it real. Attitude plays a major role in how one feels about what one is doing. This is true in all endeavors, and it is certainly true in ministry. The young man mentioned previously is a case in point. The goodwill his church members had for him made little difference in how he felt about them and his ministry because he did not believe it was there. It was there, and is there almost always. Not every church member wishes his minister well, and wants her minister to succeed. But the majority do, providing a solid foundation on which to build good ministry.

Church Members
Have Big Hearts

Here's another true story. A minister retired after serving a church for forty years. The difficulties related to succeeding someone who has served a congregation for this long are fairly obvious even to a casual observer of church life. The person who was finally called to fill the position had been in ministry long enough to know what he was facing. It was reliably reported that soon after receiving the call he commented to a ministerial colleague that he was going to see to it that the church members forgot his predecessor ever served them.

It was more than a stupid comment. It was more than a comment that revealed an ego unbefitting one ordained by the church for ministry. It was a comment rooted in an appalling lack of understanding of human nature. It was a comment that left no doubt that this minister had no idea just how big the hearts of church members can be. The fact that a minister leaves a church does not mean the hearts of those who have known and loved him immediately grow cold. Nor does it mean they should never want to see him again. Nor does it mean that should they want him to return to the church for some special occasion that their love and support for the new minister are in jeopardy.

Experience suggests that there are many ministers who do not believe that church members have the capacity to love more than one minister. How ironic, given the fact that love is one of the qualities Jesus said would reveal to the world that we—Christians—belong to him (John 13:35). How is it that love among Christians is so fragile that church members must segregate loving one minister from loving another? Who is kidding whom? Perhaps the truth is that ministers who want church members to sever their relationship to former ministers, and ministers who are threatened by the love church members have for colleagues on the same staff, simply do not understand human nature and do not trust the gospel. They may also suffer from a serious problem of inward insecurity and low self-esteem.

Unfortunately denominations often nurture this kind of neurosis. My own denomination promotes a code of ministerial ethics that discourages ministers from having any reasonable contact with members of a former pastorate. The word *reasonable* is used intentionally here. There are examples that can be cited of former ministers staying in contact with church members to the point of disrupting the leadership of the new minister. But there are also numerous instances when very reasonable, one might even call healthy, contacts between former ministers and church members occur. Yet denominational officials sometimes fail to distinguish healthy contacts from unhealthy ones.

An egregious example of this failure happened to a friend of mine. He moved from a church where he had served as associate for seventeen years to an interim position. The senior minister had also left the church. A family contacted my friend through a funeral home director to ask if he would hold services for a family member. He told them he could not, and the family needed to contact the interim senior minister. They tried to do so, but he was out of town. They called back and asked Tom if he would reconsider. He did, but finally was able to talk to the interim minister about it. This man was in full support of Tom's going ahead with the funeral service, since he did not know the family at all.

The judicatory in this area was also in an interim period. The interim judicatory official heard about Tom's holding this service and wrote him a letter of reprimand, charging him with a violation of ministerial ethics, stating that this letter would be placed in his permanent file.

This is an example of precisely what Philip K. Howard calls the death of common sense in his book by the same title (Random House, 1994). Howard's thesis is that we are a society living under the illusion that for every problem there is a law, rule, or regulation that can solve it. In the process he says we have eliminated the one indispensable element that makes things work—human judgment. Process, he says, has become more important than outcome. "Law itself, not the goals to be advanced by law, is now the focus" (p. 49).

Howard's book is mostly about government, but the church is no different. The goal of ministerial codes of ethics is to educate ministers about proper conduct, especially in the area of contacts with former church members. But the decision of the judicatory official in this situation flies in the face of this goal. Nothing was done wrong here. Appropriate ministerial ethics were observed. But a "rule" was violated. It seems the spirit of the "rule" was overlooked.

The point here is certainly not to encourage contacts between church members and former pastors, especially regarding ministerial functions, such as funerals and weddings. There are appropriate ways for a former minister to limit and/or participate in such events. Our primary concern is simply to suggest that church members have bigger hearts than ministers often give them credit for. In the long run their big hearts can take care of many of the issues ministers get caught up in, if ministers would just let church members love them as much as they have the capacity to do. Church members can support the ministry of one minister while loving another. The failure of ministers to realize this is as big a problem as any ministerial ethics violation, and can ruin what might otherwise have been effective ministries.

A woman associate who had served in the same congregation for several years recently went through a difficult conflict with her senior colleague that was rooted in this problem. He was aware that the congregation wanted her to remain in her position when he accepted the call. She told him that she was satisfied in her associate role, had no interest in moving to a senior position in the future, and would seek to support the direction in which he wanted to lead the church.

Two years later she found out that her colleague had taken steps to have her salary removed from the new budget, effectively ending her ministry at the church. He had said nothing to her about what he was doing before or after he had initiated the move. His actions did not produce the results he wanted. He succeeded only in creating such tension between the two of them that both ended up submitting their resignations.

When the dust settled, it all came down to the fact that he believed the church members were so emotionally attached to her that they never really accepted him. The truth is that only a very few of the members took sides either way. The majority of them supported the whole ministry and were shocked to discover there was a conflict in the staff. Toward the end the situation got nasty, with him openly criticizing her in his last sermon, a violation of ministerial ethics of the worst order.

This minister's basic problem was that his perception of the capacity of the church members' affections was skewed by his own emotional needs. He created an environment of competition for their affection that was unnecessary and unfair to his members. They were ready to love him when he arrived, but he was not secure enough within himself to see just how big their hearts were.

Consider another situation very much like the one above. The woman staff member had been at the church about the same length of time as the one above when a new minister came to the church. After four years they are continuing to work together, and each has a genuine appreciation and trust of the other. In comparing the two multiple-staff relationships, one key difference stands out. The new minister in the second church is an experienced pastor. The ministry he left to assume his present position was a very difficult and stressful one. He could have come into his new ministry threatened by the affection and love the church has for his colleague. Instead he had the emotional and professional maturity and stability to realize his church members had hearts big enough to accept and love him without having to reject his colleague.

It is sad and destructive to churches and ministers when ministers cannot trust the hearts of their members to have enough love to go around for everyone. Some church members have personal needs that have blocked the gospel from working in their lives sufficiently to transform their hearts into healthy loving. But these are the minority. Most of them have big hearts that can love more than one minister the same way they trust ministers can love more than one church member. Good ministry is possible when ministers believe this is true.

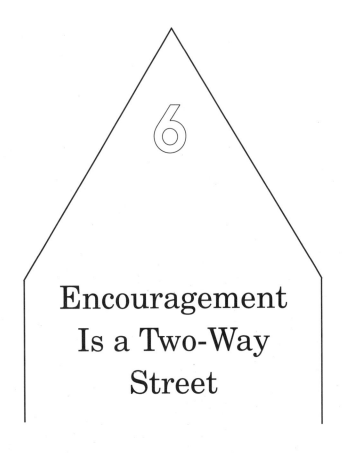

Encouragement Is a Two-Way Street

In *What Ministers Wish...* we discussed the fact that a few encouraging words to ministers can go a long way in helping them feel like what they are doing is worth it. Not that ministers have to have a pat on the back to stay in ministry. That ministry is a "holy calling" is what sustains ministers. But some encouragement along the way helps.

What church members wish ministers knew is that the same thing holds true for church members! A little encouragement can go a long way in keeping them engaged in the church's life. Encouragement is something no one gets too much of, but which many people get too little of. Most church members, like most ministers, do what they do in the church out of a sense of commitment to Jesus Christ and to the well-being of their church. They don't seek encouragement. It is not something they necessarily even think about. But they would not be human if it didn't feel good when it comes their way.

It is sometimes surprising to ministers how much their opinion of church members, and how they respond to the efforts of lay leaders, matters to the members. Most people need a measure of approval from others. Some people need a large measure of it. But all of us generally respond favorably to affirmation and support. Even a little praise once in a while is not bad, kind of like having your back scratched or your shoulders rubbed. Who doesn't enjoy that?

Church members sit in a position of support in the church. They are not the designated leader. The one who is ordained is. This fact makes it very important for ministers to express appreciation and support for the presence and work of church members. A central part of leadership is providing the encouragement followers need in order to continue their involvement.

Some people don't like the analogy, but I like to think of a congregational minister as a coach. The best coaches are the ones who encourage their players. This doesn't mean they don't work them hard or maintain high standards of performance. It means that they know that a large percentage of any game is mental, and encouragement is indispensable in developing the right attitude among the players. Personal experience has shown me how destructive failing to encourage can be. It seems funny now, but when it happened it wasn't funny at all.

In college I was a starting quarterback for a football team that could be justly described only as not very good. At the time we were a division one school, but our caliber of play seldom matched our opponents. My university still maintained the now all-but-forgotten model of "student athlete." Because we had classes six days a week, it was not uncommon for players to attend classes on Saturday morning and then play a game that afternoon.

This particular year we were worse than usual, working on a winless season. About halfway through the schedule we traveled to upstate New York to play the University of Buffalo. We had a very enthusiastic pre-game warm-up. Everybody was ready to go. We felt good, and knew that this was the day we moved into the win column. After the pre-game workout we went back into the locker room to wait for that key moment when the coach's pep talk was over and he would tell us to go out and win this one. The room was quiet. Our coach paced back and forth in front of us. There was an air of excitement. He stopped, turned and looked at all of us for a moment, and then said something I will never forget: "Well, guys, I just want you to know that you are the laughingstock of the state of Virginia!"

You could visibly see the air go out of our sails. It was like getting hit in the head instead of being patted on the back. We might not have won that game anyway, but the coach's remarks made sure we didn't. He may have been trying to work some kind of reverse psychology on us. If so, it didn't work. We went out a discouraged bunch of football players, and we ended up playing that way. You should have heard his "pep" talk at halftime!

The body of Christ has to function as a team in order for the whole body to be healthy. Encouragement is something church members need and appreciate. Ministers can easily forget that their function is to call forth the best that is in their church members, and part of doing that is being an encouraging influence in their lives. A church member not long ago said that one of the ministers in her church had a way of killing the spirit of the worship whenever it was his turn to give the benediction. She said she felt like he was saying that the people were a sorry bunch, but should go out and serve the Lord anyway. She acknowledged that they might be a sorry bunch, but it would be nice if he would say something encouraging to them once in a while. They needed to hear it, whether he wanted to say it or not.

It doesn't take much energy to encourage other people. Ministers know how much it means to them when church members take the time to say a word of encouragement to them. Every minister ought to return the favor. Encouragement *is* a two-way street in the church.

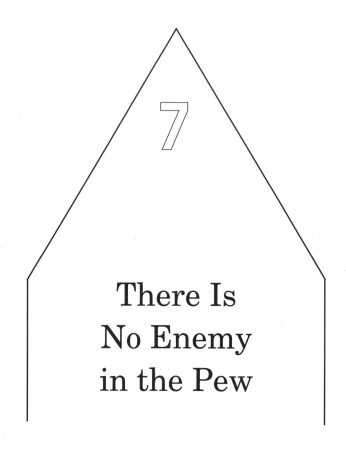

There Is
No Enemy
in the Pew

In 1965 Pierre Berton wrote a book entitled *The Comfortable Pew*. Berton was a former Anglican priest in Canada who had left not only the priesthood, but the church as well. The General Board of Religious Education of the Anglican Church of Canada asked Berton to write the book from the perspective of one outside the church looking in. Specifically, Berton understood his task as follows:

> ...to take an outsider's point of view [of the Anglican Church] and say as frankly as I wished what was wrong with it; to sum up the various widespread criticisms of the Church in plain, easily understood language; and to lay the groundwork

for the continuing dialogue in which the church might undergo the painful but necessary process of ruthless self-examination. (Preface to the American Edition, p. ix).

Berton was convinced that the primary problem in the Anglican Church, and all churches for that matter, was apathy. His assessment was that the church was filled with comfortable people in comfortable pews who resisted the church's engaging in serious issues such as the nuclear arms race, racism, secularism, social justice, and others. Institutional religion, he wrote, was a shackle to the Christian philosophy and ethic that Jesus had in mind, and that it attracted people different from the kind that followed the original precepts of the faith. Moreover, the church had become fossilized by its efforts to maintain and preserve its established place, and, thus, the church was not in the real world (p. 115).

The book was an instant success, by far outselling any Canadian religious publication up to that time. In general it was well received by the clergy, not as generously received by the laity. Some clergy suggested that the book was more about the "silent pulpit" than the "comfortable pew," but for Berton the pulpit was silent because of the power of the comfortable pew.

While he didn't come right out and call the laity the enemy, the term fits the attitude the book has toward them.

Two years after Berton's book was published, Daniel Walker, a United Methodist pastor, wrote a book entitled, *Enemy in the Pew?* Walker's book was an indirect response to *The Comfortable Pew*, and others written in a similar tone, such as *God's Frozen People* by Mark Gibbs and T. Ralph Morton, published in 1964. Walker acknowledged that the "comfortable pew" existed for many laity, and that many others were among "God's Frozen People." At the time, though, his book was intended to help the laity see the great challenge and satisfaction that come with being Christian. But he was also writing to clergy in the hope that the laity might "be understood by their ministers" (p. x). The need still exists!

The sixties and early seventies was a time when severe criticism of the church, i.e., the laity, was strong and frequent. Some of it was legitimate. The church's response to social problems such as racism, consumerism, and the nuclear arms race had often been either silence about or support for the status quo. Prophetic voices intending to shake up the church were needed. The prophetic critique was not the problem, however. The attitude of many of the prophets was. And still is. Also, these modern prophets were quite adept at seeing the speck in the eye of others while missing the plank in their own.

When the prophet Jeremiah spoke his oracles of doom to Israel and Judah, he spoke out of a deep and abiding love for the people to whom he spoke. He did not look upon them as "the enemy." The great Jewish scholar Abraham Heschel wrote that the prophet's inconsolable grief over the destiny of the people, and the uncompromising passion of the prophetic utterances, were an expression of fellowship and love for the people. Their anguish was the prophet's anguish (*The Prophets: An Introduction*, p. 119).

Ministers often forget this dimension of the prophetic role. They remember the call to speak the word of the Lord to a wayward and recalcitrant people, but they forget that they are not supposed to enjoy doing it. They also tend to distance themselves from responsibility for the church's problems. The church may be every bit as bad as ministers think it is. The criticisms leveled during the sixties and seventies appropriately called the church to a deeper fidelity to the gospel through commitment to justice and peacemaking. To a large extent much of what was wrong with the church then is wrong with the church now.

But ministers are as much a part of these problems as the laity. Ministers do no better at living out the gospel than the laity. There is a simple and obvious answer to why this is the case. It is called *sin*. It is all-pervasive, encompassing the least among us to the greatest. The apostle Paul (a "minister" in the early church) spoke the truth about all of us—laity and clergy—when he wrote: "I do not understand my own actions. For I do not do what I want, but I do the very thing I hate" (Romans 7:15). In the words of Pogo, "We have met the enemy, and the enemy is us."

That is why there is no enemy in the pew. We are all in the same boat. To say it in a more positive way, we are all members of the same body—the body of Christ. We are not enemies, for God's sake. We are members of the same family.

In a survey completed by laity that included a question asking them to state what they would like to tell their minister, one response was, "Visit in the homes in order to get to know us as people and as friends." Another responded, "Let the congregation know you really care." Still another said, "Be a link for the people to come to know God. Lead us in our lives, not standing behind and watching." Finally one said, "That they are appreciated more than they know." These are hardly responses of enemies in the pew.

But church members know when they are being perceived that way. And when they are, little constructive ministry can take place. Ministers who think of church members as enemies, even a few, are thinking in a way that corrupts the claim of scripture that the church is the body of Christ, and we are individually members of it (1 Corinthians 12:27). They are also thinking in a way that corrupts ministry, and gives birth to self-righteous arrogance.

The pews of every church seat church members, not enemies. The minister who thinks otherwise creates an adversarial relationship that is bound to hurt everyone involved. It is easy for ministers to let a few difficult people color their perception of all the people to the point of taking on the attitude of being "under siege." When this happens, one inevitably thinks in terms of "friend" and "foe." But that is no way to do ministry.

Anyone who has any experience in congregational ministry knows that ministry is difficult enough without making it worse by thinking about church members in this way. Ministers and church members do not always get along. They do not always enjoy each other's company. They do not always find one another supportive or helpful, and sometimes not even kind. But neither is the enemy of the other. Just as ministers would hope that church members do not view them as enemies, so laity have every right to expect the same of ministers. There is no enemy in the pew!

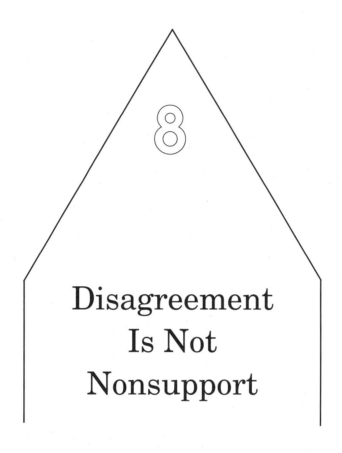

Disagreement Is Not Nonsupport

Closely related to the problem of ministers thinking of church members as enemies in the pew is their view of disagreement as nonsupport. People in general, and Christians in particular, frequently do not know how to disagree with one another. Disagreements quickly degenerate into rancor and even personal attack. Hurt or hard feelings and broken relationships sometimes become the aftermath of disagreements in the church. It doesn't have to be this way. In a community of the beloved of God, disagreement without contentiousness should not only be possible, but ordinary. And the people who should be leading the way in modeling how Christians can disagree are ministers. Some do. There are ministers who know that disagreements are commonplace because people are people. Such ministers know how to respond to disagreement without turning it into personal attack.

The rest of the story is that there are too many ministers who equate disagreement with nonsupport. They think disagreement is a personal attack. They get hurt and very often nurse the wound. They begin to distance themselves from church members who disagree with them. These ministers view church members who think for themselves and do not support every idea they suggest as if they are thorns in the flesh, even troublemakers. These ministers may not be openly hostile to church members who disagree with them, but in private they do not hesitate to express their anger about them. It is not uncommon to find them hoping that members who disagree with them will leave the church.

One minister who has been in the same church for almost thirty years has, during this long tenure, held this attitude about church members who have disagreed with him. He has been a creative and innovative minister. His vision of church has provided a biblical foundation for significant changes in the church over the years. These changes have not been without cost, however. Tensions have been high during each period of change. This minister thrives on this kind of stress. He believes the resistance to change validates the need for it. Each time, there have been church members who finally chose to leave and go elsewhere. Perhaps it was the right thing for them to do. But the minister's response has always been the same in each case. He has viewed their leaving as something they probably needed to do, since in his mind they could not support what he was trying to do.

This minister is a strong and capable leader. He holds strong convictions about the rightness of his leadership for this church, and most people who know the church would agree. But within the ranks of friends and strong supporters there is a consensus that he interprets agreement with his ideas as support and, thus, disagreement as nonsupport. What may be more disturbing than this is the fact that he would take strong exception to this assessment of his way of dealing with people. Yet a colleague who has disagreed with him from time to time through the years, but who considers himself loyal and supportive, has been viewed, by the senior minister's own admission, as unsupportive, contentious, and probably needing to leave the church.

It is rather common to find the ministers who equate disagreement with nonsupport the last ones to realize this is what they are doing. They genuinely believe that people who disagree with them do not support their ministry and are up to no good. It is very difficult for them to understand how someone can be supportive and at the same time disagree with them.

This is the kind of "drawing the line in the sand" thinking that divides churches. It makes the sheep of the church the minister's supporters (read "those who agree") and the goats the minister's nonsupporters (read "those who disagree"). Nothing lastingly hopeful or constructive can come from this kind of thinking in ministry. Any minister who falls into the trap of drawing lines between herself and church members is in the long run doing a lot of damage to the church—and to the way all ordained ministers are viewed. Church members deserve better. The ordained ministry deserves better. The whole church deserves better. If a church member draws a line between himself and the minister, the minister simply must not allow it to define how she acts toward that church member. For the clergy no line is acceptable in defining relationships. There are no lines in the church, only circles; circles that need to be big enough to encompass all who want to be in them, whether they agree with us or not!

Church members have the right and obligation to think for themselves. Disagreement is part of the process of making good decisions. Sometimes church members express views that ministers should challenge, but modeling disagreement means doing so without creating an adversarial relationship. Support does not depend upon agreement. Certainly it can happen that a church member will express nonsupport by opposing everything the minister seeks to do. There is little a minister can do in this situation beyond trying to remain open to a change in the person's behavior. But these church members are few in number. The majority who take an active role in their church do so because they support their minister. When they disagree with him, that is not saying the support is gone. It usually means they want to think for themselves. That's all. Ministers need to remember this. Everybody will be better off if they do.

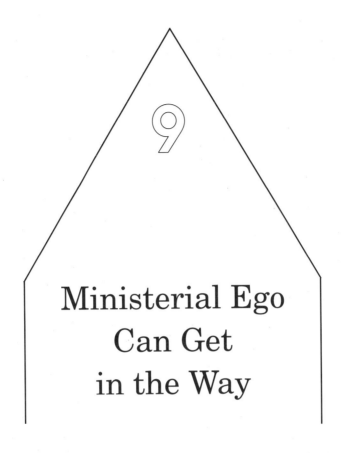

Ministerial Ego Can Get in the Way

Most ministers have strong egos. In fact, most leaders do, which is one of the reasons they are leaders. This does not mean that ministers don't feel called to ministry. It doesn't mean there are no ministers who suffer from the opposite problem of low self-esteem and a weak ego. It simply means that most ministers, especially effective ministers, have strong egos. But there is a problem. Ministers sometimes allow their egos to get in the way of effective ministry.

The human ego is defined as that part of the mind that is conscious of being distinct from others. This is the part of the human personality that controls our behavior. The ego can express healthy self-love, yet lead us to act in ways that express concern and care for others. But the ego also has the potential of negative qualities, of moving from self-love to self-centeredness, from self-esteem to self-conceit, from concern for others to a preoccupation with one's own ideas and interests. The shift can be subtle, but when it happens it is obvious to everyone around us. It is not always obvious to us.

Leaders and competent professionals usually have strong egos that sometimes, if not often, cross the line between ego and egoism. In truth it happens rather frequently. It is not a pretty sight when it does. Arrogance and conceit, insensitivity and intolerance are all children of egoism. It seems that the intellectually gifted and multi-talented people are the most susceptible to egoism. Perhaps they have a difficult time tolerating people who are not as quick or able as they are. I have known a few who, despite their giftedness, have an excessive need for approval and attention, and when they receive such they become even more infatuated with their own importance. In some instances these persons begin to believe they are absolutely indispensable to whatever task they may be involved in, or whatever cause they may be championing.

When ministers fall into egoism the church in which they are serving is in for a troubled ministry. Some years ago a large church of my own denomination called a minister I knew by reputation. Soon after he began his ministry I had the occasion to ask a member how she liked her new minister. Her reply, reflecting her small town upbringing, was straight and to the point: "I think he's a braggart!" She hit the nail on the head. His reputation was just what she said—someone who would manage to insert into any and every conversation all the things he had done, all the accolades he had received. He was quick to give his opinion on any subject, whether solicited or not. In ministry it was his way or no way. He knew what needed to be done, and seemed to resent any idea that was not his own. He lasted less than two years at the church. Yet he was able to get another pastorate about a year later.

The problem of egoism among ministers goes to the heart of motivation for ministry. At our best, those of us in ordained ministry love and serve God before anything or anyone else. Separating our own ego needs from this commitment is never easy or even reliable. Also, sin has a habit of distorting our self-perception enough to prevent us from recognizing when we have crossed the line. But it can be done. It is done by many ministers. Those who manage to keep the balance between ego and egoism are those whose prayer life is vital to their daily schedule. Here is where the best "therapy" for ministerial egos takes place. Ministers whose prayer life is deep confront the question of motivation honestly and regularly. For these ministers the "why" of ministry is as important as the "what" of ministry. This is something ministerial students have to learn. When students begin their studies their interest and focus are usually on "what" to do in ministry and "how" to do it. But it is just as important for them to learn "why" they do what they do, for two reasons. One is that the "why" keeps them going when the "what" isn't going very well. Second, the "why" challenges them to keep asking questions about their motivation for ministry. The reasons they do what they are doing can strengthen or diminish the quality of their ministry. Those who understand this to be true are the ones who serve the church faithfully. The others serve the church for themselves.

Many church members have a wonderful capacity of seeing through ministers whose egos keep getting in the way of ministry. They recognize when ministers are more interested in self-advancement than in the good of the church. And they grieve over it. Church members want more for the church. They want more for the minister. But the only person who can do anything about the problem is the minister. It begins with the recognition that the line between a healthy ego and egoism is very thin indeed. The former can contribute to high-quality ministry. The latter can virtually destroy it. This is something church members want every minister to know, for their sake and the sake of the church.

Ministry Is More than Doing What the Minister Wants

Let's add another caveat to what church members wish all ministers knew about this business of the attitude of ministers toward church members. It has to do with the ministry church members have by the very nature of being members of the body of Christ. One thing experience has convinced me of is the fact that the ministry of the laity is not a concept that has been tried and found wanting. It is a concept that has not been tried—at least not in any major way.

Ministers talk a lot about everybody having a ministry, for which there is considerable biblical basis. The call to discipleship is a call to ministry for *all* Christians. When the apostle Paul used the human body as a metaphor, he was stating in dramatic fashion the indispensability of the ministries of every church member. To say the church is the body of Christ is another way of saying everyone has a ministry. When ministers preach and teach that the laity are called to ministry, they are preaching and teaching the Bible.

The problem is that many times it is ministers who keep church members from doing their ministry. Not because they don't want the laity to have a ministry. The problem is in the way many ministers interpret the ministry of the laity. For them it means doing what the minister wants them to do, and in some cases, what the minister *tells* them to do. This is how it works.

A minister goes to a church and begins meeting with the committees, departments, etc. Soon the minister has his agenda for each group. Their task is to follow the minister's agenda. In this scenario ministerial leadership means outlining the program for the church and then urging the laity to make it a reality. And for the most part laity are quite willing to do precisely this. The church members might make suggestions here and there about how to do what the minister wants them to do. But it is the minister who sets the direction.

In this kind of church the laity depend on the minister to tell them what to do. Only it often happens that what the minister outlines for these committees to do doesn't get done—for obvious reasons. People seldom get excited about someone else's agenda. Once in a while a member will find the task exciting, and will work hard to get it done. Others will work at various levels of efficiency. When a program has a deadline to meet, it is not uncommon for the minister to have to come in and pick up the loose ends that have not been done.

Ministers and churches limp along this way for several years. Clergy try to find out the latest program someone has developed and then attempt to get their church members to give it a try. Finally, when the minister and, in many instances, the laity begin to run out of steam, the minister will seek a position somewhere else. The frustration level is usually very high among ministers who think the laity's role is to do what they call on them to do. In one situation church members simply stopped attending the "ministry" meetings they had been attending. The minister was angry and discouraged. Had he taken the time to do some self-reflection, and to talk with his church members, he would have understood what had happened.

When he began his ministry at this church the "ministry" groups were reasonably active. Attendance at group meetings had been constant for several years. Members had begun to understand and take seriously the concept of the call to and gifts for ministry among the whole people of God. Rather than continuing this focus, the new minister outlined in detail the programs he wanted each ministry to do. Some of his ideas were good ones. But within two years the ministries had virtually stopped functioning. What was the problem? The members didn't see any reason to meet. The only thing the minister wanted them to do was what he said. On several occasions a particular ministry group decided to pursue its own sense of direction. The minister resisted their efforts. Rather than fight, they gave up.

While this case may seem extreme, it reflects the reality in many churches. In my first pastorate there was a minister at a church in the same town who would not allow any committee in his church to meet unless he could be there. Through the years I have met more than a few ministers who function this way. In one region of my denomination there was a regional minister who, in his role of helping congregations find a minister, attended every meeting of every ministerial search committee of every congregation in his area of ministry. The issue for this minister was, of course, that of *control*. He was afraid of losing control over congregations, as if he actually really had it.

For ministers who function this way the ministry of church members independent of the minister stirs anxiety in them. To allow a group of church members to plan and dream and function on their own in a ministry is too threatening, so these ministers try to control the laity. There are some ministers who actually believe that ministry means trying to do everybody's ministry, and that if ministers don't do this church members will think they are not doing their job.

Ministers like this interpret the call or appointment to the church as a mandate to come in and get things going. Teaching the laity about their ministries, and taking the risk of letting them falter and fail as part of the process of learning, is simply too much of a risk. So they proceed to take over. It can be subtle and manipulative, but in the end the effect is the same. The ministry of the laity is truncated, or killed outright. There is a different way.

The Church of the Savior in Washington, D.C., has been following a different way since its birth almost fifty years ago. In 1948 Gordon and Mary Cosby began to call together a few people who wanted to take the ministry of the laity seriously. Since then the Church of the Savior has given birth to numerous ministries, and now sister worshiping communities, led by laity who assume ultimate responsibility for them. The key has been the nurture of the call and gifts for ministry among the church members.

While the Church of the Savior is different from traditional congregations in significant ways, its commitment to taking seriously the ministry of the laity challenges all ministers to do so. This brings us back to where we started. The ordained ministry is called to equip the laity for *their* ministry. This is how the body of Christ functions. The Head is Christ, who calls all church members to ministry. Clergy have the opportunity and responsibility to teach them that this means more than simply supporting what the minister wants done. It means discovering their specific call and then learning how to have the time of their lives following it.

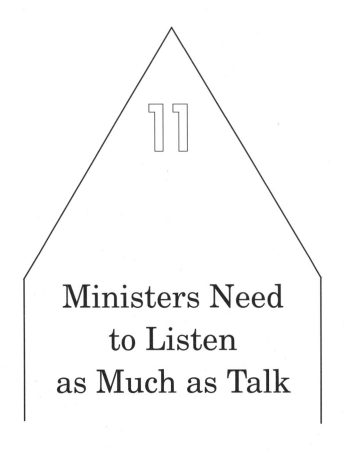

Ministers Need
to Listen
as Much as Talk

Talking is a minister's trade. Ministers get paid to talk. Most ministers I know like to talk. Ministerial meetings are not given to much silence, although nearly every minister has at one time or another wished that all the other ministers would shut up!

There is good reason ministers talk. Once in a while they have something to say. Indeed, every week they are *supposed* to have something to say when they preach. Not that all ministers do. But that is what is supposed to happen. When it comes to tasks other than preaching, ministers are supposed to have something to say worth hearing as well. Some ministers do. Many times ministers need to say something worth saying in meetings because the issues being discussed are too important not to say something.

What church members wish, though, is that, despite the need and importance of talking, ministers would realize that they need to be able to listen as well as talk. This is something that is much harder for ministers to do, although many ministers do it well. But there are more than a few who don't know what it means to listen. In addition, there are ministers who think they listen when they don't. These ministers often do more harm than good in churches precisely because they are too busy talking to know when they are being helpful and when they are not.

About halfway through the semester in a recent course I taught, I began to describe the class as students who didn't ask questions; they only made comments. That was another way of saying that some of the students in the class didn't know how to listen. They held strong views about certain functions in ministry, and were too busy disagreeing with what someone else was saying to give enough time to listen to that person. It is a common problem among people in general, and ministers are no exception.

What exacerbates this problem for ministers is the fact that they are the very people others expect to be able to listen. Churches want their minister to have something to say when speaking to them, but they also not only expect, but need their minister to listen. A significant amount of time in good ministry is spent listening to others. The minister who does not listen will shortchange his or her church members in this essential dimension of ministry to them.

In his book *The Gift of Listening* (Chalice Press, 1993), Robert Brizee speaks of the deep longing in all of us to be heard. Everyone needs to be heard, he says, and *nearly everyone can listen*. Ministers ought to be among those who do. Brizee calls listening a gift:

To listen to another is to offer a gift.

To listen with caring to another person is to offer a gift of awareness.

To listen with acceptance to all facets of another person is to offer a gift of healing.

To listen with patience for new ways to see the past events of another person is to offer a gift of freedom.

To listen with reverence for new becomings emerging within another person is to offer a gift of grace (p. x).

This is a description of the best kind of ministry anyone can offer, and the kind of ministry church members need from their minister. Listening is not the only thing a minister needs to know how to do, but it certainly is a basic skill that affects almost everything else a minister does. Listening *is* a skill. That is, it is something that is learned. It takes discipline until it becomes a natural response to another person, which may take a lifetime of discipline. Personal experience has convinced me that poor listening gets ministers into trouble more often than most other things ministers do or don't do.

Brizee says further in his book that listening can shape a community's life, when he suggests that congregations ought to become listening churches:

Listening offers something special and deeply needed by all of us. Persons can come to know that they will not be silenced, disregarded, discounted, or neglected in any phase of their church life. Rather, they will have the enhancing and warming experience of being heard, taken into account, and cared for (p. 116).

A listening church would be an environment that invited the evoking and claiming of gifts of ministry among all the members. People need to know they are valued and heard before they risk becoming involved in ministry. Only ministers who know how to listen can lead a congregation into becoming a listening church. As one laywoman put it: "Laity often are poor listeners because the minister has not set the example by listening to them." In a world of noise in which people often feel discounted and unheard, what a refreshing experience it would be to belong to a church where ministers and church members together listen as much as they talk!

Staff Conflicts
Hurt More
than Ministers

The following scenario is based upon an actual situation.

A church calls an associate minister for whom ministry is a second career calling. After a few years as a pastor of a small church he accepts the call to this larger church. Almost from the beginning he and the senior minister, who is six years from retirement, begin to have conflict. The associate is charismatic, and is very capable as a preacher. The senior minister is a good pastor and preacher, but does not possess a charismatic personality. He has served the church for eight years, and expects to stay until he retires. It becomes known in the congregation that the two ministers are having conflict. Church members begin to side with one or the other. The associate makes it known to his supporters that he would like to be the senior minister of the church.

The senior minister goes to the elders who have responsibility for ministerial staff and asks them to ask the associate to leave. After months of discussion they consent to the senior minister's request. Controversy breaks out in the Official Board over this decision. Harsh words are exchanged between members. Six months later the senior minister is asked to resign by the elders, eighteen months before his retirement. He leaves embittered and hurt. It takes several years before this church even begins to heal from the hurt and pain caused by these two ministers.

That is the way it often happens. Conflict develops within a ministerial staff, they cannot or will not resolve their differences, the conflict spills over into the church and soon the congregation is divided. At best people are upset and angry. At worst the church goes through a split.

Conflict is something that is a general problem in multiple staff churches. Ministers get hurt when this kind of conflict develops. So do church members. So does the church, and the church's witness in the community. Seldom does anything constructive come out of conflict in a multiple staff church. In the face of it church members wish ministers cared enough about the negative effect staff conflicts have on a church to work harder at resolving them. After all, the gospel does speak of the ministry of reconciliation (2 Corinthians 5:17–20), a message ministers of all people ought to know well. Church members quickly become disillusioned that people who are ordained ministers cannot be reconciled to each other enough to stop the open conflict that is hurting their church so much.

In these kinds of circumstances church members have every right to demand that ministers give an account of themselves in light of the gospel of Jesus Christ. Unfortunately church members get caught in the conflict, letting themselves get pulled in to one side against the other. It is true that church members should not take sides in staff conflicts, and are responsible for themselves at this point. What is more true is that ministers should never put them in the position of doing so. But even that is not enough. Ministers should make sure this kind of dividing up sides does not happen. Ministers can do this. All they have to do is to tell any church member tempted to take sides that it is inappropriate to do so, and that taking sides in a church means everyone loses.

Ministers in conflict can make a commitment to each other not to participate in dividing up sides. They can also covenant to try to stop this kind of division whenever they see signs that it is beginning to occur. If ministers in conflict were willing to put the church before their own needs and agendas, they just might end up seeing that their conflict is not as irreconcilable as they think it is. They might even begin to believe that the gospel of Jesus Christ should shape the way they act in conflict. That could make all the difference in the world.

What church members wish their minister knew is that everybody—ministers *and* churches—gets hurt when church staff members handle conflict the way most of them do. Energies are drained, creativity is stymied, passion for the gospel is diminished, and overall good ministry simply does not get done. What is worse is the witness ministers make to church members when they get in destructive conflict. How could it do anything but lower the respect for all ministers, and for the ministry in general? In the scenario cited earlier, the ministers who have served the church since the split have consistently encountered a strong distrust of ministers among the members.

It is not surprising. Many times ministers involved in destructive conflict persist in believing the rightness of their side of the issue justifies their actions that continue to alienate and divide. In their wake lie churches who are living examples of the fact they seem determined to ignore—that staff conflicts hurt more than ministers.

Ministerial leadership requires various kinds of sacrifices. One of the important ones is a radical commitment to reconciliation that transcends the need to be right. Certainly there are times when ministers hold such divergent views about church and ministry, or when there is a violation of trust, that makes working together difficult. There are ways to handle such circumstances that are consistent with the gospel, and ways that are not. Here is where Christian character and commitment become the real issues. And here is where ministers should serve as role models for their church members. Anything less will hurt ministers *and* church members.

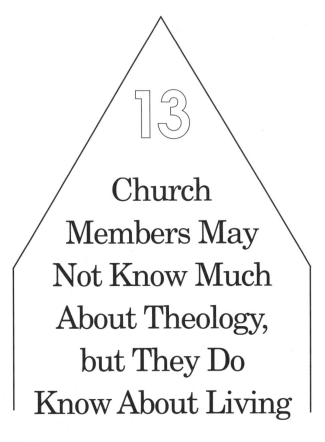

Church Members May Not Know Much About Theology, but They Do Know About Living

Most church members know very little formal theology. While the names of Luther, Calvin, and Wesley may have a familiar ring to them, most church members cannot say much about what these giants of church history preached and wrote. Most likely they have never heard of Schleiermacher, Bultmann, Barth, Bonhoeffer, Tillich, and others. Most of them could not describe the difference between systematic and process theology or between liberation and feminist theology if their life depended on it.

As far as the Bible is concerned, when it comes to the source theory of the Pentateuch, or what the Pentateuch itself is, they are completely lost. They probably assume that Paul wrote all the letters in the New Testament attributed to him, and that the author of the Gospel of John was the disciple John. They may know that Mark was written before Matthew, but they don't really care.

For the most part church members have only a cursory knowledge of just about anything and everything that is the staple of theological education today. But what they wish ministers knew is that they do know something about living. In this discipline many church members hold a Ph.D. They live on a level that is deep. They in fact have more than knowledge. They have wisdom. The school of life has taught them well, and they have been good students. They have not had the luxury of missing a class or missing a test. Every day they have to get up and go to school. It is not always fun. They often feel like they would like to drop out. But the demands of life don't give them this option.

Some of the wisest people I have known in the church are farmers. They live close to the land. They live with the reality of the cycle of birth and death all around them. They have to make tough decisions without much time to deal with the impact those decisions might have on themselves or others. Farmers have a view of life that is deep and wide. Not much surprises them. They haven't been trained to think theologically. But they do know about living, which in its own way is as theological as it gets.

These are the kind of people who sit in church pews. The composite wisdom about life can be amazing when ministers spend enough time being with them to learn from them. We live in an age when formal education is thought to be essential for anyone to be taken seriously. Many church members have had many years of formal education. Some have had very little. But the majority of them know a lot about real living, and have much to teach their minister about leading people.

It is easy for clergy to assume that because their church members have not had formal theological training, they have little understanding of what the church is supposed to be and supposed to do. Any minister who takes the time to talk to his or her church members discovers how untrue this really is. Few laypeople know the theological terms to use in talking about the church and ministry, but their insight into people is often a reliable guide regarding what to do and not do for the minister who wants to lead the church effectively.

Years ago a ministerial friend would meet a group of men from his church every Monday morning for breakfast at the local McDonald's. This was something his predecessor had done. The men invited him to join them and he thought it might be a good idea to do so, being new and all, even though he really didn't want to. He said that it didn't take him long to realize that indirectly he was getting excellent practical advice about how to lead that church from the conversations he had with those men.

This is one example of the kind of wisdom church members have about living, local customs and traditions, and political and cultural realities that ministers need to be aware of. One of the seminary's Doctor of Ministry graduates developed a resource manual for helping students and others who serve churches in the Appalachian area to understand the social, economic, and cultural life of the region. Several pieces of the material were written by laypeople.

Tapping the wisdom of the laity about living does not minimize the importance of the minister's theological reflection on church and ministry. It is only to say that knowing about living is also a resource for effective theological reflection, and here church members have a lot to offer.

Church Members
Can Think Too

Some of the smartest people in the world happen to be church members. Not all smart people are church members. Not all church members are smart. But a lot of church members are also very smart people. You would think that all ministers would know this. You don't have to be smart to know it. Common sense (something we shall discuss later) is all that is needed for any minister to realize that many church members who sit in the pews on Sunday and serve in and through the church during the week are pretty smart people. Yet there are ministers who think church members are as dumb as an old stump. They don't make it obvious that this is what they think. But they do think it.

The truth is that most church members have average intelligence, just like most ministers. Some are way above average. Others fall below the line. But whether smart, not so smart, or somewhere in-between, church members are intelligent people who can and do think for themselves. They should be treated as if they do.

By now many ministers reading this chapter are probably asking, "What's the point?" After all, ministers have enough sense to know that church members have sense, that church members can think on their own. Well, it may be true that ministers have enough sense to know that church members have sense. What is not so true is that ministers as a whole treat church members like they know they have sense. On what basis is this charge made? Consider this.

Ministers are an educated people, for the most part. Most denominations require a minimum of three years of graduate level theological study for ordination. In some traditions ordination candidates have to pass several exams before they are approved.

Good ministers spend a lifetime in study in order to do high-quality ministry. The demand of weekly preaching, for example, is one of the great intellectual challenges any professional faces. Each week ministers have to prepare sermons that have something to say worth hearing. Not all are up to this challenge. But all meet the challenge with integrity more times than not. Sometimes the sermon itself does not reflect the amount of study that has gone into preparing it. Sometimes it reflects too much study and not enough application. Whether the sermon is good or bad, though, ministers spend a lot of time in study.

Yet most ministers fail to share the tools of their learning with their church members. Indeed, a good argument can be made that the responsibility for the theological failings of today's church members lies at the doorstep of ordained ministers. Ministers have not shared with church members the kind of scholarship that has helped them grow and develop theologically.

A colleague recently spoke to a group of church members on methods for interpreting scripture. She walked them through the kind of methodology she teaches her students at the seminary. The response was openly enthusiastic. She helped them to ask a simple question, for example, to begin their interpretation of a text: "Who was the audience?" They were fascinated at the difference this question made in how they understood the text. She offered them food for thought and they ate it up. Afterward one of them came up and asked rather pointedly, "I've been in this church all my life. Why haven't I heard this stuff before now?"

A very good question. One she needed to ask her minister. Why had he not taught her this kind of approach to Bible study, or some other that he uses? Why had he allowed his church members to remain ignorant of the kind of scholarship that is learned in seminary? It is a question many ministers need to answer. Theological education is the best kept secret in the church. And the people keeping it to themselves are ministers who often complain about the lack of theological sophistication of the laity. How can they hear if there is no one to speak?

There are many reasons ministers have not shared the benefits of their theological education with church members. One of them surely is a distrust in the laity's capacity to think theologically, or to think at all. Sometimes laity will complain that ministers are talking over their heads, which ministers usually interpret to mean that they need to be more practical and less theological. That is a shortsighted interpretation. In all probability what is happening is that the minister is using just enough theological jargon to be confusing, but not enough to be clarifying. The best scholars can speak plainly without sacrificing scholarship. It is the poor scholar who confuses. Church members neither want nor need less theology. They want and need more. And when it is presented in an effective way they respond enthusiastically to it.

Church members want ministers to know that they can think just as well as ministers. The primary difference is that ministers are the ones who have had the education. They need to trust that church members will find it just as helpful as they do. This is why Charles Bayer, now retired after a lifetime of effective congregational ministry, wrote in his book *Building a Biblical Faith* (Chalice Press, 1994): "if layfolk were told what goes on in seminary classes many might be refreshed, liberated, and relieved" (p. viii). He goes on to ask if ministers have not misread the best layfolk around them who hunger for something deeper and richer than what they are getting. Bayer's sentiments are not only echoed, but charged with a sense of urgency by theologian John Cobb in his book, *Lay Theology* (Chalice Press, 1994), when he says he sees "little hope for any of our oldline denominations if laypeople do not take up the theological task" (p. vi).

God has not chosen to bless only a few with the capacity to think. The church is full of people who can think. It is time ministers started giving something worth thinking about.

Church Members Don't Grow on Pablum

Building on the previous chapter, what happens when a minister views church members as adults who can think for themselves? Leadership becomes a greater challenge. That's what happens. It is no longer acceptable, if it ever really was, to be superficial or to fly by the seat of one's pants. Meetings have to be prepared for. Sermons and study classes have to be prepared for. The minister has to be careful about what she says and does because what she says and does will be taken seriously, will be evaluated for its intrinsic merit. What happens when a minister views church members as adults who can think for themselves is that the inadequacy of theological pablum (infant formula, for those too young to remember "Pablum") is exposed. The minister begins to feel the weight of the awesome responsibility of helping church members become mature Christians.

It *is* an awesome responsibility! The last thing any church needs are members who are immature Christians (not to mention immature ministers). Some church members act like they want to be immature, and will resist attempts to help them grow up. Most of them, however, want to grow up. But they need help. They need serious help. More than that, they expect it. Giving help is the role of ministers. The minister's role is not, as we have previously said, to judge how good a Christian a church members is. It is, rather, to help church members to mature in their faith in, understanding of, and commitment to Jesus Christ as Savior and Lord.

If there is anything faculty could teach seminary students that would provide lasting help to them in everything they do in ministry, it would be for them to run scared of the responsibility they face as ministers. Ministry is all about helping people in their relationship to God. Is there anything more awesome or frightening than that? For people of faith this is the primary relationship they have in life. It is the first of all things (Matthew 6:33). Both Testaments declare that no person or thing can come before this relationship without terrible consequences.

Most ministers would agree that physicians in general, and surgeons in particular, and brain surgeons most especially, carry a heavy responsibility for caring for the lives of their patients. But many of those same ministers fail to realize that their responsibility is no less heavy. It is the heavy responsibility of caring for the souls of their church members.

Physicians see to it that their patients benefit from the best medical information available to those physicians. Ministers face a similar challenge. They must see to it that their church members benefit from the best theological information available to those ministers. Ministry calls for the deepest thinking of which a minister is capable. Nothing less is adequate for what church members need, want, and many times expect from their minister.

That grown-ups cannot grow up on pablum suggests a very practical twofold challenge to ministers—study and preparation. There is no substitute for study in ministry. Church members need the fruits of this ministerial labor. One of the best pieces of practical advice I received from one of my professors when I graduated from seminary was not to let everything else crowd out time for regular study. It has been one of the things that has guided me in ministry. Nothing takes the place of study for ministers. High-quality teaching, preaching, and overall leading is beyond the reach of the minister who is negligent in study. Ministers have various excuses for not studying, but what it finally comes down to is the minister's personal discipline. The truth about all of us at all times is that we have time for the things that matter the most to us. Ministry is no different. When a minister believes study is not only important, but indispensable, she will have the discipline to study.

But study is not enough. Helping church members grow requires good preparation. Whether it be for a committee meeting, a church school class to be taught, or a sermon to deliver, study benefits only the minister when time is not devoted to good preparation. Preparation is that time devoted to moving information out of the minister's head and heart into an organized presentation that can be understood by church members. This does not guarantee that they will benefit from the minister's study, or even appreciate it. But experience suggests that many of them do understand and do benefit. All of them have the right to expect their minister to prepare well for ministry. At the same time it is this commitment to being well prepared in ministry on all occasions that gives the minister a sense of integrity. The great nineteenth-century preacher, Phillips Brooks, told the students at Yale in 1877 in his Lyman Beecher Lectures on Preaching that the first necessity they faced was, "Be faithful, and do your best always for every congregation, and on every occasion" (p. 101, Phillips Brooks, *On Preaching*). He also noted Cotton Mather's statement to the effect that "...the best ministers in New England ordinarily would blush to address their flocks without premeditation" (p. 101).

Every church has its share of members who would prefer to feed on theological pablum. They do not want to grow or to be disturbed out of their complacency and mild religion. But every church also has its share of members who want to grow and mature. They in fact hunger and thirst after righteousness, and know that knowledge is one way to satisfy that hunger and quench that thirst.

This is what the best-selling author Thomas Moore says accounts for the unexpected popularity of his book, *Care of the Soul*. In an interview, James Newby, Executive Director of the Yokefellow Institute, asked Moore how he accounts for the success of the book. Moore responded, "I ask that question all over the country, and what people tell me is that they are hungry for something deeper than what they usually get—people are ready and willing to explore things without being given simple answers" (*Quarterly Yoke Letter*, December, 1994).

This is precisely Charles Bayer's reason for writing the book noted in the last chapter. Many of the people Moore has met *are* church members. They are the people for whom ministers need to study and prepare. They expect nothing less than the minister's best. They believe their spiritual life can grow with good guidance from their ministers. These are the members who set the standard for ministry. They want, need, and expect help in maturing as Christians, something every minister should know.

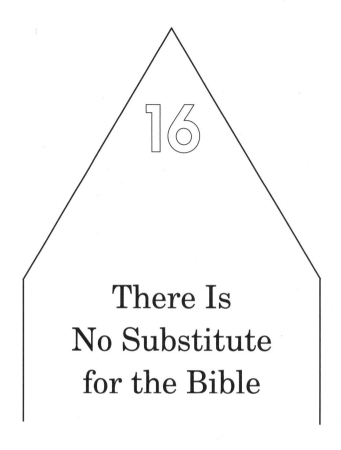

There Is No Substitute for the Bible

The Reverend Billy Graham has a habit of holding an opened Bible in his hand as he preaches. It is a familiar scene to see him with the Bible in one hand and the other hand raised, index finger pointing to the audience, making an emphatic point about what the Bible says.

Contrast this scene with what many of us see every Sunday morning in our churches. The minister will often have an associate or a layperson read the sermon text, the Bible is usually closed (sometimes it is left open if read from a lectern), the minister sets his sermon notes or manuscript on the pulpit, and begins to preach.

Say what you will about the Reverend Billy Graham, but people believe he preaches the Bible. Ask church members if they believe their minister preaches the Bible, and at best you will get a halting, "Yes...." Many times they will say their minister gives opinions rather than preaching from the Bible. Some church members will volunteer that they are not sure their minister even believes in what the Bible says, must less preaches the Bible. In most instances they are wrong. Their minister does believe in the Bible. She just doesn't worship it.

Bibliolatry is a serious problem in the church these days. This is the problem of worshiping the Bible alongside, and in some case in place of, the God of the Bible. Bibliolatry does much harm in the church, as any idolatry always does, because it distracts from faithfulness to God. Bibliolatry does not know the church's story very well, especially the fact that the church lived without the Bible as we know it—and prospered—for several centuries. Ministers should be quick to challenge the use of the Bible bibliolatry represents.

But the dangers of bibliolatry should not become an excuse for ministers to abandon the centrality of the Bible in the church's life. The Bible *is* the church's book. It tells the church's story through the claims of God on the people of Israel and the people who became the followers of Jesus of Nazareth. We may debate and argue our different interpretations of the Bible, but something ministers ought to know is that nothing—absolutely nothing—should lead them to minimize its importance for the vitality of the church at a time when the church needs all the help it can get.

Oldline Protestantism is not in the best of health these days. There are many reasons why this is the case, and there are no quick cures to all that ails us. But there is one thing that mainliners can and must do, and do it now! We must reclaim the Bible as the church's book for mainline Protestantism, as it once was. Mainline ministers have allowed fundamentalists to take the Bible from us. The contrast noted earlier between the Reverend Billy Graham and most mainline ministers stands as a symbol of what has happened. The Billy Grahams of the church are believed to be Bible-believing, Bible-preaching ministers of the gospel. Mainliners are believed to be holders of opinions about the Bible. It is not always true, of course. But perception is reality for most people, and this view of what has happened to mainline ministers is a pervasive perception. And mainline ministers have no one to blame but ourselves.

There is a compelling truth about the Bible that one could argue is critical for effective ministry. It is that there is no substitute for the Bible. That is to say, there is no source of authority from which a minister can draw to support his ministry that holds the position of authority the Bible holds in the minds of most church members, mainline and otherwise. This is a truth many mainline ministers find hard to accept.

At our seminary, senior students write a paper that reflects their own theology as they come to the end of their years of formal theological education for the basic degree in ministry. One section of these papers has to address the issue of authority. While all our students usually acknowledge that scripture is one source of authority for their ministry, it is common for them to name experience as the primary source of authority, with reason and church tradition thrown in here and there.

Testimony from their churches suggest that students quite frequently use experience as their primary source of authority in sermons. Once in a while they will quote from a book that has been helpful to them. After tolerating this for a while, church members are likely to suggest to their student that what would be more helpful is a sermon that helped them understand what the Bible says. Some students get the message. Some do not. And what is the message? It is what we have already alluded to—there is no substitute for the Bible as the primary source of authority in ministry.

As one who now sits in the pew, I better understand what for many years I have heard church members saying. It matters little to me what my minister may think about a particular issue unless her opinion springs from an honest wrestling with scripture. This is especially true if the issue is a controversial one. When she helps me hear the challenge of scripture on the subject of the morning, then I am better equipped to know how to live as a Christian in this crazy world of ours. Fortunately, our congregation had this kind of minister before she resigned. We are now in a search for a new one. We can only hope and pray the next minister of our church will share the same commitment to scriptural authority.

Despite what some ministers believe about church members, the truth is that when scripture speaks, church members listen. They at least listen to scripture more than they do to anything else ministers use for authority. It is often said that church members do not want to be disturbed, and that change comes slowly, if at all, in the church. In fact I think I have said that as much as anyone. But what needs also to be said is that difficult issues can be addressed and church members will think about them if and only if the minister seeks to approach them from the best interpretation of scripture of which he is capable. The minister who tries to challenge church members to faithfulness without honest and open use of the Bible is a minister who will fail.

Nothing commands the attention of church members like scripture. All a minister has to do is to test this thesis to find out how true it is. Of course some church members will not respond to scripture no matter how much a minister uses it. Some church members will immediately respond in affirmation to the use of scripture. Most will listen, taking their minister seriously, but remain initially unconvinced about the implications of the text for their lives. This is why it is so important for ministers to use the Bible frequently, regularly, relentlessly, as the primary source of their authority. They have no other source that can be as persuasive as scripture can be over a period of time. Why? Because there simply is no substitute for biblical authority in ministry. The Bible sets the standards and boundaries for the church's life. There are voices to the contrary in mainline Protestantism today. They are voices church members have enough sense not to listen to. They can only hope their minister does, too.

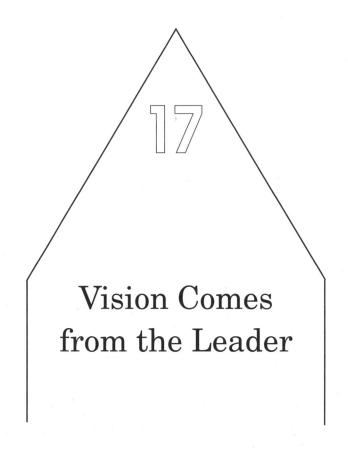

Vision Comes
from the Leader

The word *vision* is defined as "unusual competence in discernment or perception; intelligent foresight." In his classic essays, *Servant Leadership* (Paulist Press, 1977), Robert Greenleaf defined better than most the importance of vision for effective leadership. Writing about the qualities of the leader who is servant first, Greenleaf wrote:

> A mark of a leader, an attribute that puts him [her] in a position to show the way for others, is that he [she] is better than most at pointing the direction (p. 15).

Greenleaf goes on to say that this pointing the way is rooted in the ability to have vision or foresight. It is this vision or foresight that is the "lead" of the leader. Once lost the leader is no longer able to point the way (p. 22).

The Bible makes the claim that where there is no vision the people perish (Proverbs 29:18). All of which suggests that vision is essential to any group's life. The church is certainly no different. The church in all its various and wondrous forms has to have vision in order to have direction.

Church members have the right to expect that vision for the church will come from their minister. Presuming a leadership steeped in scripture and tradition, ministers have the responsibility of providing the overall vision for the church. Church members play a pivotal role in how this vision is lived out, but it is the minister who, as Greenleaf says of leaders, must point the way. The minister who cannot do this is not a leader, and should not pretend to be.

Giving vision to the church is not only a responsibility in ministry. It can be an exciting challenge. Yet so many ministers are missing this boat. One reason is their own provincial understanding of the church that keeps them from thinking big enough about the church. There are few ministers whose vision is too big for the church. The opposite is more the rule. They have a vision too small for a church facing the end of the twentieth century. People are not drawn to small vision. They are drawn to that which stretches and challenges them. Ministers who can raise people's sights to a new way of thinking about Christian living in the modern world are desperately needed; ministers who have a vision wherein inclusion rather than exclusion defines the church, where risk rather than playing it safe is valued, where Jesus as Lord of the church determines the church's values and priorities, where meaning is rooted in the truths about life the Bible teaches. This is a vision every minister who thinks big enough will hold up before her people.

Some ministers miss the vision boat because they want to climb the hierarchical ladder of success. Not much vision comes to one who is caught up in the need to

74

succeed and to have power. Moreover, when it does there is a reluctance to speak out of that vision when it challenges the success and power of those who are listening. It is sometimes the case that vision will challenge denominational interests and priorities. Ministers who want to move up the success ladder will find it troubling to speak out of such vision because of the jeopardy it can pose to such movement. Ministers with vision do not always get with the denominational program. There is a price to be paid for following vision, and some ministers decide it is not worth paying it, especially when their families suffer along with them.

Some ministers miss the call to provide visionary leadership because they do not live deeply enough into scripture. The Bible issues a challenge to contemporary church life at almost every turn. Church members and ministers alike are in constant need of being reconverted to the gospel. Keeping the machinery going, climbing the denominational ladder of success, trying to keep the church ship afloat is hardly what the gospel is about. Yet it is so easy for all of us to fall into these ways of thinking and acting. The church needs leaders who offer a fresh word, who shake us out of our complacency and comfort, who call us to renew the covenant to belong only to God. Church members are up to this challenge. If anything, many churches have members up to a challenge much greater than what they get from their ministers.

Ministers ought to be able to provide clear direction for the church. That is a minister's primary responsibility. Vision, foresight, even insight—these are the lead of ministers who can point the way for today's church. Ministers do not have all the answers. But they do have a role to fulfill in the church, and the primary one is being a leader. Where there is no vision, not only do the people perish, but the minister wastes their time while they do. Church members not only need visionary leadership; they want it. Every minister ought to know this. More than that, every minister ought to give it.

Running Too Far in Front of Church Members Leaves Them Too Far Behind

As important as vision is to ministerial leadership, most church members I know want to speak a word of caution here. It is that being a visionary minister does not mean running so far ahead of church members that they cannot hear what their minister is saying. Leadership includes a commitment to staying with those being led, no matter where they are. A leader can be so confident of the vision that is his lead that he runs so far ahead of the people that they cannot follow.

This is especially true regarding issues of controversy. The strident voices among ministers who chastise church members for not agreeing with them on issues seldom help lead the church to deeper faithfulness. Convictions, as important as they are, can be used as an excuse for a lack of will in living with and loving the people ministers are called to lead. That is a breach of trust, if not ministerial ethics. The story of the child in church listening to the sermon who asks her mother why the preacher is so mad at everybody points to the problem of leaders who allow their vision to turn them against the people they are leading. Commitment to justice ceases to be just when its voice is self-righteous.

Part of the challenge of visionary leadership is trusting the work of the Holy Spirit to make the vision winsome. It is the Spirit that empowers people to follow, not the eloquence of the leader. If the vision is clear enough, the leader has to be willing to trust its power. Its fulfillment may take a lot longer than the leader wants it to take. But this does not mean the people do not want or need the vision. It just means the leader must speak it with love and patience.

It is this kind of love and patience that tests a minister's understanding of what it means to lead as a member of the body of Christ. As true as it is that "not much happens without a dream," and "for something great to happen, there must be a great dream" (Greenleaf, p. 7), it is equally true that visionary leaders can become critical and unloving because the people they lead are not following close enough. The tough part of visionary leadership is being able to stay close enough to the followers to be heard by them.

What happens when leaders run too far ahead of their followers is that a deep sense of disenfranchisement develops that can easily grow into resentment and anger. This is the mood of the nation at this present time. If the congressional election of 1994 says anything at all, it says that when people feel disenfranchised long enough, they eventually vent their frustration and anger. Thus voters threw out the Democrats who were viewed as those in power. The word from the electorate was, "You are not in touch with us so we want some new leaders." And if the Republicans don't listen, then they will be thrown out as well. It matters little at this point whether the Republicans can do any better, or even whether they will lead the country in the right direction. The point is that people are not willing to follow leaders who run so far ahead of them that they lose touch with what the people they are leading really think and feel.

In the church this kind of situation strikes a fatal blow to any ministry. Ministers who get too far ahead and so far out of touch with their members will one day look back and realize no one is following. What is perhaps worse, the vision will be damaged. The church suffers, not because the people have no vision, but because the visionary has destroyed the vision. There is a case to be made that this is part of what has happened in oldline Protestantism. Denominational leaders are seen by church members as out of touch with what is really happening at the local level. Church members feel disenfranchised. They feel ignored, unrepresented, and criticized. It may be that denominational leaders have a greater vision of the church than most church members, but that is not the issue. The basic problem is in knowing how to lead, not where to lead.

Ministers should lead people in the direction they believe God wants them to lead. But *how* they lead is as important as where. Leading has to take place among the people, not way out in front of them. Church members cannot catch a vision of the church from a minister they believe has lost touch with them. They need to know their minister cares enough to stay with them, talk *to* them rather than *at* them, and understand that following is not any easier than leading.

No one has to make a case for the fact that mainline/oldline ministers are often considered by their church members to be more liberal than they are. The nature of theological education is reason enough to believe that this perception is based on fact. At the very least ministers who catch the spirit of the gospel's concern for the poor and the marginalized, who believe the good news is about *in*clusion rather than *ex*clusion, will find themselves a few steps removed from where many church members are in understanding what it means to be a Christian and to be the church. A few steps are OK. The steps turning into leaps and bounds is what undercuts ministry. There is no way to lead people the leader has left behind. That is a principle of leadership every minister ought to know.

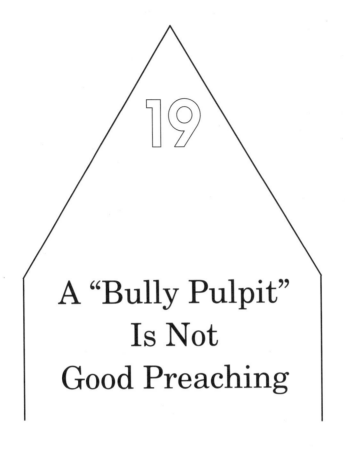

A "Bully Pulpit" Is Not Good Preaching

The great preacher and teacher of preaching P.T. Forsyth once described the church as the great preacher in history. He went on to say that "...the first business of the individual preacher is to enable the Church to preach....He must preach to the Church from the Gospel so that *with* the Church he may preach the Gospel to the world" (Quoted in Stuart W. McWilliams' *Called to Preach*, St. Andrews Press, 1969, p. 4; emphasis added). Forsyth went so far as to call on the individual preacher to be a sacrament to the church in order for the church to be a missionary to the world.

This suggests that preaching is a sacred and holy task. Ministers have the awesome responsibility of preaching to the church. It is tempting not only to talk *at* church members, but to preach at them as well. The minister who preaches at her people no longer understands what it means to preach. Theodore Roosevelt may have been correct in calling the office of President a "bully pulpit," but nothing could be further from the truth than to think preaching is a "bully pulpit." Church members have found that almost all the time a "bully pulpit" in the church is occupied by a bully! This is not somebody church members want to listen to, and not somebody the church needs to preach. Ministers are called to preach in a way that bridges the gap between the pulpit and the pew, not widens it. This is the only way a preacher can equip the church to preach to the world.

A "pulpit" becomes "bully" when ministers use it to vent their frustrations and anger at church members, push their own political agendas and self-righteously champion causes. Excuses for this kind of preaching abound. Usually it is the sorry state of the church that justifies it, what with selfishness, inhospitality, and "isms" of all kinds so prevalent. That the church is in a sorry state cannot be denied. But ministers are part of the church, and hold equal share in its glory and in its sins. Jesus' prohibition about casting stones applies as much to preaching as to the circle of folk ready to stone the woman caught in adultery.

The worse thing about "bully pulpit" preaching is how far it misses the mark regarding what church members need. Some years ago Charles Kemp, a distinguished teacher in the area of pastoral care, wrote a book entitled *The Preaching Pastor*. The title suggests an attitude about preaching quite different from a "bully pulpit." Kemp wrote that preaching is much like counseling in that personal change is one of its primary aims. This change is nurtured, he went on to say, when parishioners gain new insights, make a new resolve, gain the courage to try again and receive assurance of divine resources" (p. 8). "Bully pulpit" preaching cannot nurture church members in this kind of growth and change. In truth it gets in the way of it.

This is not to suggest that ministers cannot and should not "speak the truth in love" when they preach. Preaching can have an edge to it and remain pastoral. At the same time browbeating and self-righteous—or even righteous—indignation is not necessarily speaking the truth. It does not trivialize truth or love to say that truth is love and love is truth. Truth that does not convey love is not truth, but opinion masked as truth. God is truth, and God is love. That which is of God is both truth and love, or it is not of God.

Practically what this means is that ministers are called to speak the truth they believe is the gospel of Jesus Christ—which makes it more than their truth—in such a way that church members hear the relentless love of God claiming them as God's beloved. Ministers are also called to preach in such loving ways that church members hear the relentless truth of God challenging them to do justice and love mercy. This is a far cry from a "bully pulpit." It is, rather, real and relevant preaching because it is preaching that is faithful to the gospel. This is the only kind of preaching there should be in the church. Most church members I have met already know this. Ministers should too.

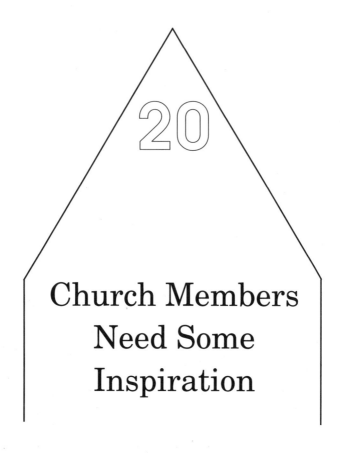

Church Members Need Some Inspiration

One of my mentors frequently used to say that Christians needed to outthink the world as well as outlive the world. He was convinced that sound thinking was essential for healthy faith. All Christians are called to love God with their minds as well as their hearts. But this is not the whole story. People have hearts as well as minds. If there is anything church members wish ministers knew it is the fact that they want and need some inspiration. They want ministers to know that touching people's hearts is as legitimate as challenging their minds.

There are several insightful meanings of the verb *inspire*: "To fill with noble or reverent emotions; to stimulate...creativity...energies, ideals, or reverence" (*The American Heritage Dictionary*, 1985). This kind of inspiration is worthy of every minister's attention and labor. Sound thinking is not enough to engender devotion to Christian living. People need to be inspired to noble emotions, to be inspired to reach for great ideals, to be so inspired by God's love and grace that they respond with reverence and humility. Perhaps no minister is capable of such inspiration, for it is the work of the Holy Spirit. But ministers can be instruments of inspiration, if not its source. Ministers can be sufficiently filled with the Spirit that their words and actions inspire others to have higher thoughts and to love with deeper devotion.

In my own experience a ministerial voice from the distant past continues to inspire me. It is the voice of Phillips Brooks. We have noted that he wrote the book *On Preaching* based upon his Lyman Beecher Lectures on Preaching delivered at Yale in 1877. It is one of the most inspiring books I have ever read. Though it is focused on preaching, it is much more a book about the minister and the nature of ministry itself. Brooks obviously was a man of great intellectual strength, but his words reach more than the mind. They touch the deepest level of the heart. His words and thoughts inspire me to noble emotions, to creativity. Each reading renews my energy for ministry.

In almost thirty years of ministry there have been some low points. These moments have made me wonder if ministry was really worth the sacrifices involved, worth the all too frequent frustrations, disappointments, and personal hurts that seem to accompany working with people. In such low moments the call that first inspired me to enter ministry fades. The great challenge of preaching the gospel loses its appeal. This is when I have pulled Brooks's book from the shelf and read through it once again. It has never failed to help me regain my balance, to lift my spirits, to renew my faith in the rightness of my calling and the nobility of serving in Christian ministry. In short, the ministry of Phillips Brooks now a century and more in the past continues to inspire me through his words of wisdom and hope.

Would that all ministers would be able to inspire in this way. Not all ministers, of course, have been so endowed with the gifts and abilities of a Phillips Brooks. But all ministers can be vehicles for inspiration that influence and even change people's lives. This is because the Holy Spirit works through the lowliest of those who have been called to ministry. The power for inspiration is not of our own making, but is of God. This was certainly the conviction of the apostle Paul, who wrote: "We have this treasure in earthen vessels, to show that the transcendent power belongs to God and not to us" (2 Corinthians 4:7, RSV).

Church members today are hungry for inspiration. They want their spirits lifted and their hearts moved. They are wondering what is wrong with ministers who seem so uninspired themselves. They can tell their minister is not excited about ministry. They know ministry is not easy, but they don't understand why the power of the gospel does not sustain the minister in spite of the difficulties. They feel like they are being asked to be devoted to the church when all the while their minister seems to have less and less energy for ministry.

Church members need something more from ministers than the usual drone of appeals for volunteers and financial support. The world is hardly a source of inspiration. Not that they expect the church to provide an antidote to the difficulties of daily life. But they do expect the church, and specifically ministers, to speak a different word about love and service, about compassion for others, a word that offers an alternative view of reality, a word that inspires them to believe that at its core life is good. It is a reasonable expectation that every minister ought to take seriously.

Why is inspiration so hard to come by these days in the church? It would be easy to blame church members themselves because of their infighting and nitpicky ways. But that is too facile. Ministers like Phillips Brooks are not exempt from frustrations and discouragement. They are able to inspire in spite of these things. No minister can justifiably blame church members because he offers little or no inspiration for deep devotion to Jesus Christ, to the church, or to service in the world.

The problem lies with the minister, not church members. Ministers who do not inspire have a spiritual problem. They are not living deep enough into the Spirit themselves to be inspired in order to inspire. Most likely they are trying to do ministry by their own power. It never works. Consequently they give in to the pressures of ministry and lose heart. The solution is to call themselves back to prayer. Here is the ultimate source of the minister's inspiration. Even the eloquence of a Phillips Brooks needs the heart of a minister who prays in order to inspire. Prayer is the link connecting the heart of the minister to the heart of the gospel, and it is in the gospel that ministers find their true inspiration.

Ministers need not fear emotionalism in trying to inspire. To seek to inspire as we have defined inspiration is never manipulative. Manipulation is self-serving. Genuine inspiration is not. It seeks to direct the devotion of church members outward to one another and into the world. It is not self-serving. It calls us to service. Mainline/oldline ministers have been unduly cautious about trying to inspire because of their disdain for excessive emotionalism that sometimes characterizes charismatic ministry. Church members do not want ministers about trying to manipulate them. They simply want their hearts warmed and their spirits lifted. What they want is something the gospel of Jesus Christ ought to do—and will—when it is proclaimed by one who is passionate about it. They want to feel the truth of the gospel as well as think about it. They want it written on their hearts as well as on their doorposts. They want ministers to help them raise their sights. They want to be shown the way to be connected in mind, heart, and spirit to God and to others. They want to hear a word of assurance that helps them believe when it doesn't make any sense to believe. In short, church members want and need some inspiration from their ministers. One can only hope that more and more ministers will want—and even need—to give it to them.

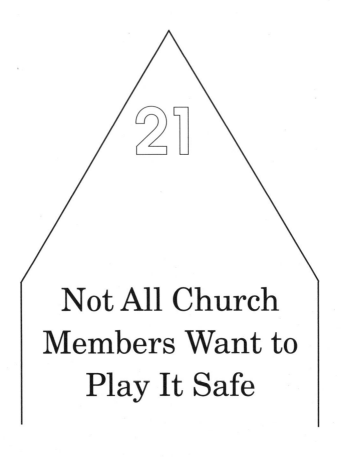

Not All Church Members Want to Play It Safe

In *What Ministers Wish...* reference was made to a statement by Charles Bayer, at the time minister-in-residence at our seminary, who described the church as a lifeboat in which all the people are huddled together in the middle in order not to create any waves. This description is provocative in several ways. The church of today does often act afraid and tentative in its ministry. The mood of survivalism seems to control decisions by congregations and denominations. And it is not just church members huddled in the middle of the boat. Ministers are there as well.

Not all ministers, of course, are trying to play it safe. There are many courageous ministers who live out their ministries with integrity against great odds. But what these ministers—and all ministers—should realize is that there are many church members who have the same kind of integrity of commitment as Christians. They don't want to play it safe in the church either. They want the boat to move ahead. They are less afraid of making waves than of growing stagnant and irrelevant. They know that the church is not called to play it safe or to support the status quo. They may not be anxious to jump headlong into the fray of every battle that comes along, but they are not unwilling to take risks.

Because we are prone to over-generalizations, ministers frequently talk as if all church members want to avoid controversial issues and resist taking stands on unpopular positions. Nothing could be further from the truth. Church members are rightly concerned about how taking risks will affect their congregation as a whole. They worry about losing people who disagree with the risk being taken. They cannot easily dismiss the potential negative financial impact on giving to their church should the congregation become embroiled in controversy. But none of this is the same thing as saying they are unwilling to take risks, and ministers who claim it is are giving many church members a bum rap.

A close friend of mine for many years has been the pastor of the same congregation for nearly fifteen years. In a recent sermon he acknowledged that he has been no stranger to controversy throughout his years in ministry. He went on to reflect on the tensions of the past year of ministry in his present church. He acknowledged that they had "lost several members who have been discontent with some of the issues we have addressed and the directions in which we have moved." He also acknowledged how uncomfortable and painful it is to lose church members for these reasons. He went on to say how thankful he was for the elders of the church who have firmly supported his leadership. Most specifically he thanked them for their ministry of reaching out "to those who are angry, hurt, or discontent, seeking to listen, to care, but also remaining centered on what the church is called to be and do."

In this congregation these elders are living examples of church members who do not want to play it safe. But they are not the only members in this congregation who think this way. The minister also expressed appreciation "for persons who have differing opinions and understandings, but choose to stay involved in the community of the church, expressing their views and remaining open to those of others, recognizing that we all have need to grow in our understanding of what God calls us to be and do."

Ministers are tempted to see these church members as exceptions rather than the rule, and to feel that there is at best a handful of members in their churches who think and act this way. What is interesting about my friend's church is that when he went there it was a moderately conservative congregation comfortable with its life and witness. They had had a stable ministry with the previous minister who had not been willing to take many risks, but who had provided effective maintenance leadership.

No one would have believed this congregation could have been led in the direction they have followed the last several years. What accounts for it? The minister's ability to lead? Of course! But something else has also been at work in this church. It is the fact that the members have always been up to the challenge of taking the risks they have taken. It's just that before now no one had asked them to take the risks they have been willing to take.

This is what every minister should consider when assessing his or her ministry. Not all ministers know how to lead a church in a way that taps the willingness of church members to take risks. And certainly not every church member is willing to take risks. But there are church members who will when the right leader comes along and asks them to do so. Indeed, as one of my colleagues has pointed out, church members care about the world too. Sometimes ministers use a few church members who resist social ministries as an excuse for not challenging the keen social conscience of the many others who are ready and willing to put their faith into action. It is all a matter of leadership.

Is this kind of leadership easy? By no means! The minister of the church previously mentioned says that the last year has been a very difficult year in his ministry. He has wanted to run away on more than a few occasions. He is at this moment trying to discern whether after so many years in the same church it is time for him to leave. But the risks he and the church members have taken together have produced several permanent changes in that congregation's life.

This is but one example of churches whose ministers and members together are taking risks in ministry. There is a Southern Baptist church that has pushed the boundaries of membership by spending several months studying and discussing how they should respond to openly homosexual persons who want to become members. Because Southern Baptists vote on people who want to join, confronting this issue has been very risky for this church, so much so that they were forced to withdraw from the local Southern Baptist association. But the members voted in an overwhelming majority that taking this risk was where they believed the Lord was leading them. A sizable number of people have chosen to sever ties with this congregation. Tensions within the ministerial leadership team have strained relationships. But the membership has made it clear that they want to stay the course and continue the risk-taking.

Another church is moving in the direction of a healing ministry. Two healing services have been held, and the response has been strongly affirming. The ministers have been the ones with the most doubts about this turn of direction. After the first service they went to the lay leadership and asked if it should continue. Their response was *yes*. Neither the lay nor the ordained leadership quite know where this is leading them. They are sure that they are not yet comfortable with holding healing services, to the point where the ministers intentionally publicize them as "Services of Prayer for Healing."

Theologically they may be correct in the phrasing, but it was not their theology as much as their lack of clearness about what all this means that led them to identify the services this way. Moreover, it is the support of the lay leadership that is giving the ministers the encouragement to continue to risk leading the congregation into an area of experience with which they have no knowledge. Listening to the ministers talk, it is obvious that they have genuine doubt about getting involved in a healing ministry of this kind. It is also clear that in a real sense they are seeking to let the laity take the lead, and they are doing so.

These are but a few of the churches that have members who are willing to take risks in ministry. Sometimes the talk around ministerial tables is so negative that one wonders if there are any church members who want something more from church than being made to feel good. Well, there are. The ministers of the churches we have discussed have found them. There is good reason to believe every minister can find them simply because people are people, which means that in every congregation there are church members who want more than playing it safe. They are willing to take the risks the gospel calls them to take. They do not lack the will. They often do lack someone who knows how to show them the way. But, then, that is not their fault. It is the fault of the very ministers who claim these same church members never take risks.

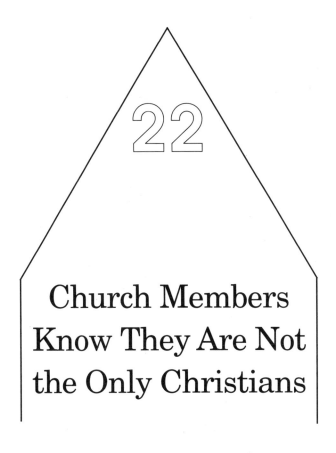

Church Members Know They Are Not the Only Christians

Ministers are often heard to say that church members don't care about Christian unity, or don't have much interest in ecumenical issues. On the face of it there seems to be more than a little evidence supporting this view. Few congregations devote much time, energy, or money to ecumenical relations and concerns. How many church members even understand what the ecumenical movement is, or that it is, is a genuine question. More to the point, denominational identity itself seems to be rather unimportant to today's church members. Ironically, though, this is one reason to think an ecumenical spirit among church members is actually quite strong. The lack of denominational loyalty, while a problem in its own right, reflects an inclusive attitude among many church members toward members of other denominations.

Only narrow-minded church members believe they are the only true Christians around. Their number is not legion, thank God. The vast majority of church members today know they are not the only Christians. Whether or not they call their attitude ecumenical, it is. It needs only to be named and nurtured by ministers, not ignored.

Yet ministers are the very ones who so often do ignore the potential good this attitude among church members can do. What is worse, there are some ministers who seem to feel threatened by the prospect of greater cooperation among Christians of different stripes. Doctrinal purity and traditions that matter little to the average church member loom large in the minds of such ministers. Not that doctrine and tradition are unimportant. But few church members I know hold rigidly to particular doctrines or traditions. Instead they adapt to the particular practices of the church they attend, even when they are very different from what they have previously experienced. This is why church members move with such ease from one denomination to another because of marriage or job relocation or personal dissatisfaction with a particular church. It is not uncommon for members of my denomination to join a church that does not serve communion each week. They may miss not partaking of the Lord's Supper weekly, but this does not keep them from placing membership in a denomination that doesn't follow this practice.

Ministers who do not name this attitude as ecumenical and nurture it toward even stronger support for unity among all Christians are missing a great opportunity for ministry on behalf of the whole church, not to mention overlooking an essential dimension of the gospel: "I ask not only on behalf of these, but also on behalf of those who will believe in me through their word, that they may all be one" (John 17:20).

While church members may not be excited about Christian unity, most of them are hardly resistant to it. On the contrary, more church members than ministers often realize struggle with the disunity among Christians denominations represent. They wonder what all the fuss is about. They realize that Christians are Christian regardless of church affiliation. In many instances they consider differences among Christians petty and absurd. A comment such as, "We're all trying to get to the same place anyway, aren't we?" is quite common among the laity. While the theology of such a comment might be questionable, the ecclesiology is not. It contains an understanding of the church as one body that is firmly rooted in scripture.

What is needed today is leadership from ministers who want to move unity to a top priority in their congregation's life. These are the ministers who can and will nurture and guide what I think my colleague, Michael Kinnamon, himself one of the primary ecumenical leaders in the world, rightly calls the "ecumenical impulses" among church members. The inclusive and open attitude of church members toward Christians of various denominational ties is their way of saying to ministers that they know they are not the only Christians. The challenge is for ministers to pay attention to what they are saying and then act on it. It takes thoughtful leadership to call forth the impulses within a congregation that are not readily apparent. Cooperation among congregations in a particular community is a good thing, but it takes intentional leadership for such cooperation to grow into a vision of unity among all Christians. There is every reason to believe most church members want this kind of leadership. The real question is whether ministers are willing to give it.

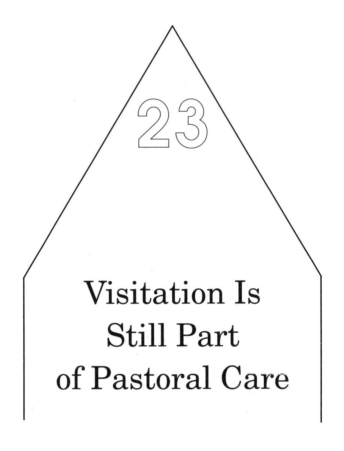

Visitation Is
Still Part
of Pastoral Care

One of the most persistent complaints of church members is that ministers don't visit. They almost never visit in the homes of active members, sometimes in the homes of shut-ins, less often in nursing homes, and inconsistently in the homes of prospective members. Ministers do better in regard to hospital calling, but even here they are not always as attentive as church members want them to be. What church members don't understand is why so ministers today do not make pastoral care through visitation more of a priority in their ministry. It is a priority for the church members who pay their salary.

The following experience of one church member illustrates the problem. Jane started attending a church near her home. After several Sundays the minister asked if he could come by to visit. She said yes. He told her he would call and make an appointment. She missed the next Sunday, but heard nothing from the minister. She returned to worship two weeks later. As she was leaving he apologized for not calling, but assured her would that week. No call came. Even though she had not requested the pastor to visit, she was looking forward to his visit so she could talk to him about some questions she had about the church. She continued to attend worship regularly, and each time he assured her that he was planning to visit. Months passed without him calling. Finally, after nearly a year had passed the minister called and made the appointment to visit. She received him graciously, and later joined the church. Less committed persons might not have done either.

The wife of a recently retired minister shared with me that their experience has been the same as Jane's. She said they have visited every congregation of her denomination in the city where they are living, and not one pastor has even mentioned a desire to come by and visit with them. It's as if these ministers don't care one way or the other whether this couple joins their church.

These situations involved prospective membership in a church, but the failure to attend to a need for pastoral visiting is a vivid example of what frequently happens in general today. Pastoral visitation, as Thomas Oden has pointed out in his book *Pastoral Theology* (Harper SF, 1983), even for sincere pastors "is among the most difficult and distasteful aspects of their work" (Oden, p. 170). He goes on to say that many ministers feel they have no time for pastoral visitation, and some "have great difficulty even pretending that calls are meaningful" (p. 170).

One thing that may account for this situation is the fact that pastoral counseling has captured the interests of ministers to the point of overshadowing the once essential role of pastoral visitation. It must be said that the increasing role of counseling in ministers' schedules has to a signifcant degree been in response to the needs of many church members who have sought out their counsel and guidance rather than paying to go to therapists. Yet many, if not most, ministers simply find counseling a more appealing form of pastoral care than visitation, especially when some of the visiting has to be done in the evenings. Becoming a pastoral counselor is one of the most often cited reasons students give for wanting to enter seminary. Many of them have been helped by such counseling themselves.

The most disliked part of ministry cited by students is pastoral visiting, reflecting what Oden suggests is a prevalent attitude among experienced ministers. Reports from churches they serve bear out their dislike. In almost all instances the primary frustration in student-served congregations is the lack of pastoral visitation. One woman recently said that one of our graduates characterized the church's expectation of pastoral visitation as out-of-date. She said he went on to say that the seminary was now teaching that whenever possible students should make appointments to meet with members at the church rather than in home visitation. She wanted to know if this was true.

There is no way to know if the student actually said this or not. If he did he did not accurately represent what he was taught. Preparing people for congregational ministry is the peculiar identity of our seminary, and without equivocation we stress to students that visitation remains an essential part of pastoral ministry. Whether students pay attention to this is another matter. In this regard the survey of recent graduates revealed that they are spending four to six hours a week in visitation. Retired ministers would laugh at such a statistic. Church members bemoan it.

What every minister ought to know is that pastoral visitation builds the relationship with church members that is the foundation for everything else the minister does. Here the minister meets her people on a more intimate basis. This is where she can articulate how the gospel speaks to the specific circumstances her church members face. Pastoral visitation is the primary way a minister serves as a shepherd to his people. It is a sacred responsibility that should not be neglected, and certainly should never be disdained.

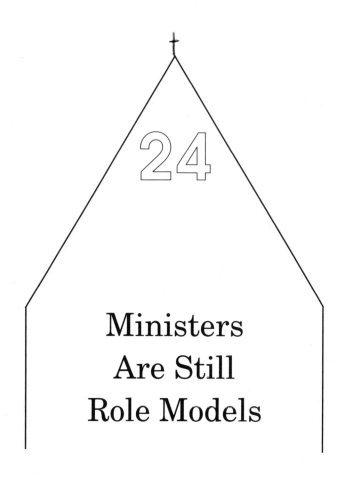

Ministers
Are Still
Role Models

De-pedestalization of ministers is in. Pedestalizing is definitely out. And many ministers seem determined to prove it. Serving as a role model for church members is something ministers have been struggling against for several years now. It is as if being a role model is an unjust burden ministers resent having placed on them. They reject the notion that church members have any right to expect the minister's life to be different from their own.

There is some legitimacy to the way ministers feel about pedestalizing. The word *hypocrisy* comes to mind when church members expect ministers to be better than they are. The hypocrisy is not so much in what they expect of the minister as it is in what they don't expect of themselves. The gospel does not make any distinction between Christians regarding lifestyles. Ministers are not supposed to live one kind of life while church members are free to live another. The gospel's call to strong moral and ethical character is no respecter of persons. Clergy and laity alike are expected to follow a narrow way that witnesses to the truth of the difference Jesus Christ makes in their personal lives.

Having acknowledged the general claim of the gospel on all Christians to live in ways consistent with the life of Jesus himself, insofar as it is given to us to do so, it is nonetheless appropriate and right that church members view ministers as bearing a special responsibility in this regard. The expectation of church members that ministers should set an example of what it means to live the Christian life should not be dismissed out of hand. Certain positions hold particular standards of conduct that are inescapable. This has become a recurring theme in the public sector where even the appearance of impropriety is sufficient for one to be dismissed or voted out of office. And who is not dismayed at the reckless disregard so many professional athletes display today for the responsibility of being role models to young people?

Like it or not, being a minister puts one in the position of being a role model. In a sermon preached in our seminary chapel, United Methodist Church Bishop Robert Morgan pointed out this fact to students. He told them that ministers have the responsibility to model Christian living, and that failure to be a role model undercuts the power of the minister's teaching and preaching of the gospel. He urged them to go out and live the gospel as well as preach it when they graduate. The bishop's words were his way of charging students who were candidates for ordination to ask themselves the question, "Have the means of grace...begun to be deeply ingrained in my lifestyle?" (Oden, p. 18).

Taking seriously the responsibility ministers have to serve as role models will never be reduced to moralism as long as we recognize the basic truths about life upon which it rests. Here the wisdom of the past states it plainly:

> The better [person] will always conquer the better cause. I suppose no cause could be so good that, sustained by bad [people] and opposed by any error whose champions were...of spotless lives, it would not fail. The truth must conquer, but it must first embody itself in goodness. And in the ministry it is not merely by superficial prejudice, but by the soundest reason, that intellect and spirituality come to be tested, not by the views [ministers] hold so much as by the way in which they hold them, and the sort of [minister] which their views seem to make of them (Brooks, pp. 50-51).

Causes do not change the world. People do. And changes that have a lasting impact on the soul of any society stem from the power of the personal character of those who lead the way. This does not mean that leaders are flawless. Indeed, the best leader is the one who knows her own weaknesses. But the ubiquitous nature of sin does not exempt a leader from seeking to embody the highest possible standard of character.

I would hope that all ministers know just how weak and sinful they are. Perhaps it is not as much a lack of will to set an example as it is discouragement in the face of their failure to do so that leads ministers to reject their role model responsibility. It is not easy to be viewed as living better than one actually does. This is the dilemma many ministers feel every day of their existence. Yet the nature of ministry leaves ministers with no alternative but to serve as models for the kind of life to which they call their church members. To ignore this reality will not only lead to personal trauma, but will cast a shadow over ministry as a whole. One bad example in ministry reflects on the calling of all.

To argue that ministers are still role models is not a call to purity, but to sincerity and discipline. Ministry today needs women and men who are committed to work-

ing at being open to "the means of grace" becoming ingrained in their lifestyle. It is not solely a matter of
sexual conduct that is at issue here, although this is an
area of growing concern among clergy. A United Church
of Christ conference minister recently commented that
upon assuming her position she was confronted with
eight clergy sexual misconduct cases. "Sex in the forbid-
den zone" (see Peter Rutter's book by this title: J.P.
Tarcher/St. Martin's Press, 1989) is something in ministry that has been ignored for too long.

Modeling Christian living, however, reaches beyond
the responsibility of sexual standards. It has to do with
core values, with the minister's attitude toward and use
of money, power, and time. Sexual misconduct always
grabs the headlines, but it is not the most pervasive
example of the failure of ministers to be role models.
Materialism may be the greatest temptation ministers
today face. While there are ministers and families who
continue to live under the burden of substandard salary
scales, there are more who have grown accustomed to
living beyond their means in order to taste of the good life
American capitalism promises.

It is probably true that money is not evil in itself, and
it also is not true that wealth disqualifies one from being
among the faithful of God's people. But it *is* true that
money is a subtle tempter whose corruption can be as
undetectable as poisonous fumes, and there are more
than a few ministers who have become its victims. When
the majority of the world's population is poor, it is difficult to understand how any minister can be comfortable
with the lifestyle many of us are living in this country.
What kind of role models are we as ministers if we in-
dulge in the "good life" when estimates of the homeless
population in the United States now reach into the mil-
lions?

This is not an attempt to put ministers on a guilt trip,
although there may be room for some legitimate guilt
surrounding this issue. The point is that ministers face a
special responsibility for living a lifestyle that reflects at

the very least an honest wrestling with the demands of the gospel in the face of rampant materialism. It rings hollow for ministers to preach the riches of the gospel in giving meaning to people's lives whatever their station in life while making sure they themselves get their piece of the American pie.

A student at our seminary is a woman who owns a successful business. She lives a comfortable life. She is also deeply committed to the gospel. A woman of intellect and ability, she offers much potential for leadership in the church. Since responding to her call to ministry, with no small amount of anguish before doing so, she now struggles to bring together the claims of the gospel and her good life. At times she thinks she should sell her business and use the money to help the poor whom she already serves in various ways. But she has a family to think about, and they have not been called to the ordained ministry. What future direction God will lead her in at this point remains undefined. But that she is asking tough questions about what it means to be a role model as minister in a poor world reflects the kind of integrity that already makes her a good role model.

This is the kind of person the church needs in ministry. There are many of them out there. They are the examples church members need in order to believe the gospel can and does make a difference in a person's life. The radical claims of the gospel apply to the lives of church members as much as ministers, to be sure. But ministers are the ones who really have no choice in the matter. Each minister must individually answer the tough questions that go with being a role model. There are no easy answers for all situations. But the one sure thing is that all ministers are called to be role models, and all should aspire to measure up. Jean Vanier, founder of L'Arche, perhaps said it best when he wrote in *Community and Growth* (Paulist Press, 1989): "The leader is always a *model*, and teaches more by what he or she lives than by what he or she says" (p. 209). Most church members know this. Every minister ought to as well.

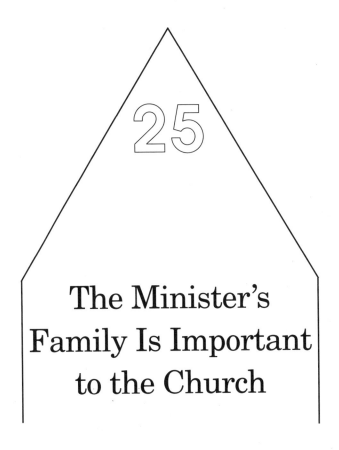

The Minister's Family Is Important to the Church

Dee Dee Meyers served as Press Secretary for President Bill Clinton, the first woman ever to hold this high-level post. In an interview reflecting on her experiences just before she left her position, she told the story of being called by the late night talk show host David Letterman. In the conversation she told him that Chelsea Clinton was off-limits to his often sardonic humor. She explained that while she believed the office of President made Mr. Clinton and, to some extent, even the First Lady fair game for the late night comics (especially with Mrs. Clinton's high-profile style), she did not believe that any President's children shared this vulnerability. She told Letterman that using Chelsea as the object of his humor would violate basic standards of decency and respect, not to speak of the unjust personal pain such humor might cause her.

The difficulties that accompany the "glass house" effect on families of public figures is something that only those who experience it can fully understand. It is tempting for those not living under these circumstances to be a bit cavalier about the pain and hurt families experience because they live under the light of public scrutiny. People often seem unable or unwilling to believe that the "glass house" is real. One would hope that the place where genuine sensitivity about these circumstances would exist would be in the church. Unfortunately this has not always been the case. Some church members have been the worst examples of violating the privacy of the minister's family.

Ministers are high-profile people. It is only a matter of degree that separates a minister from the President when it comes to living in a "glass house." The scrutiny is the same. It is the scale of the scrutiny that differs. Thus the families of ministers live with the reality that their lives are only partially private.

More than a few of them can tell stories of the outrageous things they have experienced as a result of living under these conditions. One minister's wife told of living in a parsonage that was actually connected to the church via a breezeway. Several church members had keys to the parsonage. It was not uncommon for her to hear the key turn the lock, look up, and see a church member coming through the living room door unannounced. On one occasion she was taking a bath when she heard someone in her kitchen. She hollered to see if it was her husband. Hearing no answer, she hurriedly got out of the tub, dried off, put on a robe and went to the kitchen where she found the chairman of the board "inspecting" a recent repair on one of the cabinets.

No ministerial family should have to put up with this kind of emotional abuse, which is what it is. No church that really is a church should allow any of the members to behave this way. It violates trust, respect, and common decency that should exist between the church and its ministerial family. There *are* some limits to public scrutiny for ministerial families. The church does not own the minister or the minister's family. It is a poor witness to the best meaning of Christian community when church members push beyond appropriate limits.

At the same time, when churches are served by a minister with a family, it is only natural that church members consider the relationship of each member of that family important to the church. This is especially true for the minister's spouse. At best, the expectations church members have on ministerial family members are no different than the minister's expectations of the families of church members. Each member of the family is important to the church. It would be unthinkable, if not unconscionable, for a minister to have no interest in or concern for all the members of a church family. The same thing holds true for the attitude of church members toward their ministerial family. They want to get to know each member of the minister's family. They often take pride in their ministerial family, especially in rural areas and in small and medium-size towns, introducing them to anybody and everybody they can.

This kind of role may not be the favorite thing ministerial families have to accept, but it is something that goes with supporting a spouse—and parent—who has been called to ministry. It is support that matters a great deal to any minister. Having your family to be there for you is something ministers find to be a key to effective ministry, and quite often to simply staying in ministry. It is an enigma that so many spouses have such little interest in being a participant in church life. Some hardly even attend weekly worship. It speaks of little respect and support for their ministerial spouse. It can also have a negative impact on the way church members view their minister.

In one church the minister's wife and two young children seldom attended worship. Because she worked outside the home, the members had little expectation for the minister's wife to be involved much in church activities during the week, but they did want her to be there on Sunday. Yet the leaders never raised this concern to the minister. The minister was left with the impression that the situation was acceptable to the church. After a couple of years he discovered that many people had not accepted his wife's frequent absence on Sunday. One of them finally told him that she didn't know how he expected anybody to listen to his urging of them to come to church when he couldn't even get his own family to come.

Church members may remain silent about such matters, at least for a while, but it is a serious mistake for a minister to think the issue does not matter to them. It's time for ministers to quit whining about churches thinking they are getting a "two for one" deal when they call a minister who is married. This is hardly a serious issue anymore. But church members do want a minister's family to take an active role in the church's life. In a recent survey, the members of a large congregation of my own denomination overwhelmingly supported a statement that defined the expectations of the minister's spouse as participating and providing "leadership in the life of the church as any other member does." Church members usually excuse the minister's children from such expectations, but they will not be so understanding when it comes to a spouse. Nor should they. The appropriateness of setting limits on the kinds of expectations and behavior of church members toward ministerial families should not lead to a rejection of any and all expectations. A minister's family has been—and always will be—important to the church. It's the way it should be, and any minister who does not know this does not understand much about the nature of the church.

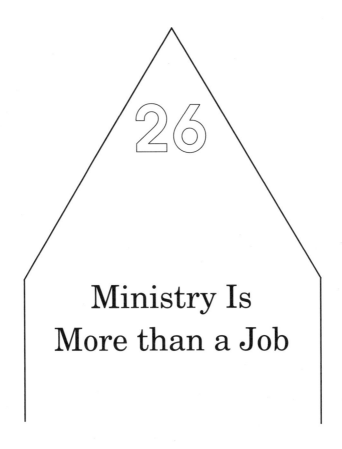

Ministry Is More than a Job

Ministry is more than a job. It is a vocation, which means it is a holy calling. The Latin root of the word *vocation* is *vocare,* meaning "call." Ministry is the process of being summoned to the service of God. One meaning of the word *call* is to summon. Ministry is not something one chooses before one is called to it. The calling involves the moment of decision when a person says *yes* to this summons, but the initiative is of God.

A *job,* on the other hand, is a task to be done. It is work to be completed, usually for pay. A job is employment, a means of earning a living. It is something that need not have any sense of "calling" to it. The relationship between the task and the compensation for it generally determines whether one does the job and how well it is done. Ministers get paid, and there is work to be done, but the pay is not the reason for doing ministry, and does not influence how well it is done. Ministers do not punch a time clock precisely because ministry is not a job. A genuine sense of "calling" has to be present. The claim of God, the summons of God, is what keeps ministers in ministry.

The key to ministry being more than a job is the minister's own attitude. And the test of attitude is time. Most ministers enter ministry with a positive attitude. They may tremble in the face of the holy calling they have received, and well they should. But they have no less zeal than fear. They believe they are doing something whose importance has cosmic dimensions. Often they are naive about what is ahead of them. It will take personal experience to bring them down to earth and into the realm of the real world. Early in ministry they want to change the world, to make a difference, to let their lives count for something beyond a moment's gratification.

It is a rare person who does not start out this way in ministry. Their attitude could not be better. But it is the attitude with which they end up that reveals the extent to which they have maintained a sense of vocation in their work. Most people in a job begin to live for retirement once it comes into sight. They are often bored with what they are doing. Some cease to show up mentally for work a long time before they retire. One of the signs of this attitude toward the job is early retirement, which has become commonplace. Some workers hate what they are doing so much that they live in the hope that their company will make retirement attractive enough that they can get out. Early retirement is not a bad thing, of course. It offers people a chance to do something else they have always wanted to do.

This is what ministry should be all the time—something a person has always wanted to do. Ministry has been described as what a person should do only if she could not be happy doing something else. That is one of the most misleading statements about ministry there is. In the first place, how do persons know if they would be happy doing something until they do it? I might be happy playing professional baseball, especially since at the moment the current players don't seem to want to play. In a questionnaire used with ministers, one stated that he had always wanted to play professional baseball. Does that means he should not be in ministry? Of course not!

The good intentions behind thinking one should not be in ministry if one could do anything else is no doubt to underscore the "call" dimension of ministry. If so, the ministry would be better served by describing it as something one cannot imagine not doing. This, of course, would not be unique to ministry. Doctors, teachers, actors, even lawyers, speak of not being able to imagine themselves doing anything else. They might be able to do something else, and be happy doing it. But they are doing what they are doing, and they cannot imagine not doing it. That is the kind of attitude that makes what one does more than a job. It applies to ministry as much as it does to other professions.

The church needs ministers who want to be ministers. It does not need people who are ministers because they cannot do anything else. Nor does the church need people in ministry who really don't want to be. The minister who feels like he is "stuck" in ministry will turn it into a "job," and probably do a lousy "job" of it besides. At the same time this attitude will not escape the notice of church members. Whether ministers believe it or not, church members know when their minister is happy and when he is not. Church members need ministers who want and need to minister to them and with them. Not many of us would want to be under the knife of a surgeon who wished she were doing something else. The same principle applies to the ministry. Not many church members want to sit at the feet of a minister who wishes she were doing something else. They shouldn't have to. It is up to the minister to get out when the dread of ministry lasts longer than a normal temporary moment of discouragement.

Ministry is a holy calling. It is standing on holy ground terrified by the mystery of what one is being called to do and by the One doing the calling. The power of the holy calling and the awesomeness of the mystery can fade when the rigors of ministry are confronted. But those who still cannot imagine not doing what they are doing—happy at the moment or not—are the ones church members will know have been truly called to ministry. For them, on more days than not, ministry will always be far more than a job. For on more days than not they know that

> There is no career that can compare with it for a moment....Its delight never grows old, its interest never wanes, its stimulus is never exhausted. It is that to which they have been summoned to do. They desire to do no other (Brooks, p. 4).

Ministers Are Not
the Only
Busy People

The demands of ministry are great. Ministers have the privilege of sharing the most intimate moments in people's lives—birth, death, marriage, divorce, illness, crisis. Multiply any and all of these by the number of members of any given church and we get some idea of the kind of demands ministry places on a person.

My home church was very large. One Easter we had two thousand people attend church school and morning worship. Our pastor served the church for fifty years. During most of that time he was the sole ordained minister on staff. The only other paid staff was the church secretary and a part-time organist/choir director.

John Suttenfield was a great man. His day usually began around five-thirty, when he would rise for prayer

111

and study. It was not uncommon for him to visit members in the hospital twice a day. The rest of the time he attended to administrative responsibilities and visited shut-ins and prospective members. In between he managed to serve as mayor of our city of fifty thousand during a period of rapid growth and development. John Suttenfield was, indeed, a great man.

Perhaps he was an unusual minister as well. Today a church the size of the one he served will have at least two, and sometimes three, full-time ordained ministers. The "senior" minister on this kind of staff will spend a considerable amount of time in study. Sometimes the "senior" will have a personal secretary who screens calls and generally protects him—and it almost always is a "he"—from unwarranted interruptions. The other staff members have a scaled-down version of this style of ministry. They are professionals, and want to be treated as such.

Certainly the demands *are* great, even in this kind of ministry environment. Church members can expect more from one minister or an entire staff than is humanly possible to do. But looking at the work done by ministers in the past who usually served alone puts the demands of ministry today in perspective. Comparisons, of course, don't tell the whole story. But they can bring a healthy corrective to what is sometimes a self-serving perception of the stress of our labors in ministry. The truth is that John Suttenfield, though a gifted minister, was typical of his generation. Serving during the post-World War II era when U.S. Protestant churches were growing by leaps and bounds, these ministers worked long hours every day, often seven days a week. They were overworked and underpaid. But they never seemed to tire of doing the ministry they fervently believed in.

There are ministers like this today. They love the ministry, and never seem to grow weary of its demands. They meet each day in anticipation of something wonderful happening. They are sometimes awed by the privilege they have to share those intimate moments in people's lives. But not all ministers feel this way, by a long shot. More than a few ministers focus their attention less on the task they are doing than on how busy all the demands of ministry make them. They feel like they are expected to do more than anyone has a right to expect, and they resent it. Ministry has become synonymous with stress. These are ministers who are doing more and enjoying it less.

Burnout has become an experience common to ministers today. Perhaps it always has been, but it's been only recently that it has become a topic for books and workshops. As busy as ministers used to be, one would expect burnout to have been a serious problem for them. But, of course, burnout does not come from being too busy. In his book *Ministry Burnout* (Paulist Press, 1982), John Sanford says that burnout is rooted in a loss of meaning, not in long hours of work, which brings us back to the issue of ministry as a "job" discussed in the last chapter. The minister for whom ministry is a "calling" does not burn out. This is because being busy does not cause a minister to burn out. Being "lost" does. That is, when a minister loses her way, begins to feel that what she is doing is not worthwhile, she becomes a candidate for burnout.

Burnout in ministry is an issue that deserves thoughtful attention. But it is not the demands of ministry that are the problem. It is a loss of meaning, which ministers can experience regardless of how busy—or not—they are. What is more, most church members are every bit as busy as their minister. They are also struggling to hold on to some meaning for their lives that transcends the often meaningless work they have to do to earn a living. The last thing they need is to be ministered to by a minister who feels the same way. Misery may love company, but it hardly ever brings light into a darkened room. Ministers, human as we are, cannot avoid the stress of their labors.

The hard truth church members wish ministers knew is that they—ministers—are not the only busy people. Everyone is busy! When a minister starts focusing on how busy he is, he has lost direction and meaning. The answer is not to figure out a way to do less. It is, rather, to find a way to do things with more meaning and purpose. In other words, the minister must find a way to bring the gospel to bear upon her own labors. That is the way out of the darkness. Church members often need to find the same way, and have every right to expect that ministers can help them find it.

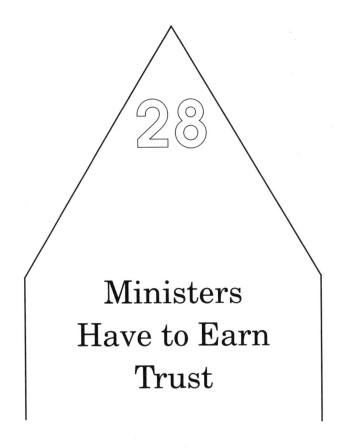

Ministers
Have to Earn
Trust

Leaders have to have followers in order to be leaders. More than that, leaders lead primarily by the consent of the led. Even in business leaders with the power to hire and fire employees still lead by the consent of those being led. Years ago a major corporation hired a college professor to head one of its division plants. This man had done some consulting work for the company that had impressed its officers. Because of problems at the plant, they let the previous vice-president in charge of the plant go. The professor seemed like the ideal candidate. He accepted their offer, giving up his tenured position at the local college. Within less than a year he was let go. The reason? Plant morale was at an all-time low. Workers had responded negatively to his style of leadership. A dramatic drop in productivity was the result. This man could not lead because those he led did not want to follow. It was not solely a matter of the workers not liking their new boss. Based upon interviews with division supervisors company executives found that there was a universal absence of confidence in this man's understanding of the plant or the workers. Simply put, the workers did not trust him.

Trust is a key factor in all leadership. In his book *As One with Authority*, Jackson Carroll suggests that the trust of church members is the foundation for authority ministers need in order to lead. This trust is rooted in (1) ministers being the representative of the sacred and (2) ministers having recognizable expertise. Says Carroll:

> If we have authority as clergy, it is because laity perceives us to be reliable interpreters of the power and purposes of God in the context of contemporary society. And this involves both spirituality and expertise, not one without the other. (p. 54)

The key to following any leader is first being able to trust him or her. Ministers have to be trustworthy in order to have church members follow their lead. There was a time when it could be assumed that church members trusted ministers by virtue of the office of ministry. This is no longer something to be taken for granted. Ministers in today's church have to earn trust. There are some rather obvious factors that have helped to create this situation. One is the publicity surrounding the hypocrisy and dishonesty of televangelists such as Jim Bakker and Jimmy Swaggart. The former lived in luxury while pleading with his supporters to sacrifice to send him money. The latter railed against sexual immorality while he was picking up prostitutes at night.

Another factor that has contributed to ministers now having to earn the trust of church members is the politicizing of the gospel by liberal and conservative preachers. Jerry Falwell and Pat Robertson are perhaps the most notorious ones, given their public exposure via their personal television programs. They peddle off old-line Republican Party agendas and rhetoric as the gospel of Jesus Christ without missing a beat, reaching a new high or low, depending on your perspective, with their latest invectives directed toward President Bill Clinton.

There are also liberal preachers who politicize the gospel to suit their personal agenda every Sunday from the pulpit. A few years ago a student preached a sermon in our seminary chapel on the issue of homosexuality. The content was his castigating of those who did not agree with his own views about the issue. So politicized was the sermon that had the seminary been inclined, fairness would have required a rebuttal sermon the next week. Afterward he rejected any legitimacy to the criticism that he had politicized the gospel in a manner not unlike people like Jerry Falwell, except the politicizing served his liberal agenda.

It does not much matter whether politicizing comes from the right or the left. Its impact on people's trust of the judgment and integrity of ministers is almost always negative. And well it should be. Ministers have been too careless in dealing with important issues from the pulpit. That such issues should be addressed in sermons is not the issue. *How* they are addressed is. Something is wrong with any sermon that needs a rebuttal for fairness, and something is wrong with ministers who persist in defending this kind of politicizing of the gospel. Church members deserve more, and they deserve better.

A third factor that comes readily to mind regarding the issue of ministerial trust is its abuse by clergy. The most publicized abuse of ministerial trust has been sexual molestation of children by clergy. Several Catholic priests and Protestant clergy have been indicted and/or convicted of child molestation, some of which occurred many years ago with victims just now coming forward.

The problem goes beyond sexual abuse of children, of course. In a widely publicized case an Episcopal bishop quit after confessing that charges were true that he had had several affairs with women in the churches under his care. These violations of ministerial trust seem to be a weekly headline.

Abuse of trust, however, has not been confined to sexual misconduct. A non-clergy friend was recently called by a member of a ministerial search committee as a reference for a candidate. The person calling began to ask her about the candidate's financial circumstances, especially whether he and his wife handled their personal finances responsibly. This friend finally asked the person why she was asking these kinds of questions. The reply was that the church had had serious problems with the previous minister in these areas.

In another situation a church lent a young minister several thousand dollars to help him consolidate school loans. He ended up leaving the church without even attempting to pay the money back. The church could have taken legal action, although they had lent the money in good faith without any contractual arrangement. They decided not to follow this course. The minister committed an unethical act that he will never have to pay for, but his successors will in the form of having to work hard to earn the people's trust. All ministers pay for the indiscretions of the few.

A more subtle factor related to ministers having to earn trust today is the gradual erosion of trust in any kind of authority, which has been occurring over the last twenty or more years here in the United States. Cynicism within the general population is the worst it has ever been. No one in any position of authority can expect to have people's trust before it is earned. And even then it can evaporate overnight. Perhaps this kind of thing is cyclical, and distrust of people in authority will give way to trust being a given once again. No matter. It isn't that way now, and that is what ministers have to recognize.

The need to earn trust does not apply only to the person of the minister. It also reaches into the quality of the minister's leadership. Here is where all ministers are again paying the price for the poor leadership of a minority. More than a few churches have followed a minister down the path of near self-destruction in the trust that the minister knew what he or she was doing. In the end they discovered the opposite was the case, but the discovery came too late to avoid much damage to the church's stability and to the future relationship between church members and minister. One church initiated a major fund-raising campaign to build a multipurpose building, what is often called a "Christian Life Center." In the process they undercut support for the yearly operational budget. In the midst of the controversy the minister resigned to take another position. The lay leadership decided to invite representatives from the church planning agency of their denomination for advice. The conclusion of a detailed study these representatives made was that the church would be taking on a project beyond their financial capacity to build and/or maintain. Moreover, it was a project that had little to do with responding to the ministry challenges facing that congregation. Here again, future ministers will pay the price of this particular minister's betrayal of trust.

What makes the need to earn trust so troublesome in the church is the fact that it is present *in* the church. The nature of the church is that of a community of people who value and practice honesty, which is the bedrock of trust. But the reality is that we live in an age of cynicism toward all authority, and we live at a time when the ministry has too often earned distrust among church members. It is not that church members do not want to trust their minister. It is, rather, that they have good reason not to. They have either had their trust in ministers betrayed or they know a congregation that has. They are afraid to take the risk of trust until they see some reason that it is justified. This is not a situation ministers like. It is not a situation most church members like either. But it is the way it is, and that is what ministers need to know, and then learn what to do about it.

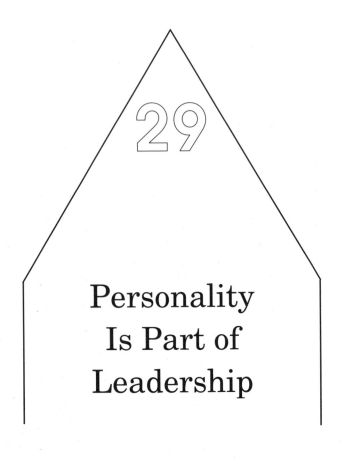

Personality
Is Part of
Leadership

To suggest that personality is important in ministry is to invite the criticism of those who are disdainful of ministers who seek to gain a personal following. The horror of Jim Jones leading more than nine hundred people to drink poisoned Kool-Aid immediately comes to mind when the subject of personality in ministry is raised. Then, of course, there is the shadow of David Koresh and his Davidian followers in Waco, Texas. Yet it is naive for ministers to believe that personality has no place and makes no difference in their leadership in the church. Church members are, as we have said, human just like ministers. So like it or not, church members generally like or dislike ministers because of their personalities.

The word *personality* means "the totality of qualities and traits, as of character or behavior, that are peculiar to an individual person; distinctive qualities of an individual, especially those distinguishing personal characteristics that make one socially appealing" (*The American Heritage Dictionary*). These definitions suggest that personality basically is who a person is, and even what a person does. Understood in this way one wonders why there would be any question about the importance of personality in ministry.

There was a time when psychologists believed that personality was fixed by the age of six, and not much changed after that. Today there are theories claiming that people continue to grow and develop into adult years, perhaps over a lifetime. The popular personality theory called the Myers-Briggs Personality Inventory, for example, says that everyone has dominant and underdeveloped personality traits, and the task is to learn our dominant or preferred traits while intentionally working on the underdeveloped ones. These modern personality theories at least give us hope that we are not stuck with being who we are without any chance of changing. Probably the truth about ourselves is that we are who we are most of the time, and with some work we can learn to act in a different way when the circumstances call for it.

What remains constant, though, is that our personality makes a difference in the way people respond to us, and how we respond to them, regardless of who we are. It is crucial in ministry for clergy to accept this fact. What is more, there are certain personality traits ministers have to have in order to be effective leaders. Much of what we have been discussing throughout this book comes down to basic personality traits ministers need to have or at least have to give the appearance of having. Among the most important are an ability to set people at ease, to listen, to be supportive without having to give answers, and a capacity not to offend.

This last one—the capacity not to offend—is not about telling the truth of the gospel. It is about things a minister says and does—or does not say or do—that create unnecessary tension or embarrassment that are rooted in a personality that is either too passive or too domineering. The minister who wants things her way all the time, and the minister who refuses to be assertive at all, both end up creating tension in a church. The minister who has social skills to the extent that they seem artificial, and the minister who has no social skills at all, will both find themselves more and more isolated from the people they are seeking to serve.

Personality is important in ministry because it either enhances or inhibits leadership. When we interview applicants to our seminary, it is not uncommon for the members of the admissions committee to discuss our personal response to the personality of the candidate. Not that we do not look beyond personality in assessing their qualifications. We find some candidates too facile, and we find others almost impossible to talk to. We then look for other qualities that might justify admission. But the personality of the candidate is an important factor for admission because it is an important part of ministerial leadership.

Doctors and lawyers and company CEOs and others may be able to function efficiently without a good personality, but this is not the case in ministry. Few ministers possess all the qualities leadership in the church requires. Even fewer of us don't encounter church members who simply do not like us. And most of us have to go behind ourselves cleaning up the messes our personalities sometimes create, and work hard at overcoming personality traits that get in the way of dealing with people. But ministers who do effective ministry almost always are people whose personality is appealing to those they lead. Personality is not the whole of leadership. It is not even the central part. But it *is* a factor that cannot be ignored. Personality may sometimes play too large a role in the way church members assess the effectiveness of their minister's leadership. But people are people, and they respond in positive or negative ways to ministers not as much because of their brilliance or skill as because of who they are. Ministers respond to church members the same. They can hardly expect their church members to be different.

Ministers
Determine
Real Ministry

Something that is real is authentic, genuine—such as a real diamond rather than an imitation. Imitations of the real thing abound in the material world. They are called imitations, but the truth is they are fakes, which means they give a false and misleading appearance. They are not authentic, not genuine. Those who market imitations try to convince consumers that a fake is just as good as the real thing. They even resort to euphemism, like a store in our city that is called the "Almost the Real Thing Store." Having almost the real thing is supposed to be as good as the real thing itself.

The subtle effect of this kind of mass marketing is that it entices people to settle for imitations. It also raises the value of the real thing as something rare, while cheaper imitations flood the market. It also leads to outrageous claims being made for the effect of having the product, whether real or imitation. The world of advertising seems to thrive on blurring distinctions between what is real and what is imitation or imaginary.

What is most interesting—and disturbing at the same time—is that the people who sell these items take on the "fake" qualities of the product they are pushing. There are more than a few instances where the imitation product seems more real than the person selling it. This is especially true when celebrities promote products they have probably never used before, but whose endorsement comes at a very high price. The ultimate casualty in this world of image making is people being real, genuine, authentic people being who they say they are, believing in what they say they believe in.

Ministry is not unaffected by this sort of thing. In an age of declining church attendance and influence, image making has become an acceptable method of church promotion among ministers. Commercials and literature abound that upon close examination have the distinct flavor of skilled marketing strategies. Ministers seek to make themselves into smooth-talking, confident promoters of the gospel. In a world dominated by consumerism, more and more ministers are turning to image rather than substance to promote their churches.

A recent experience brought this home in an unsettling way. I attended a Christmas Eve midnight worship service at a very large Presbyterian church. The church has more than twenty-four hundred members, beautiful facilities, and a large ministerial staff. It was interesting to find out during a tour of the building that the senior minister's office, located some distance from the main office, includes a bath and shower, living room, administrative office, and private study.

There was a strange sense of "theater" as we sat in the sanctuary waiting for the service to begin. The noise and mood were similar to what you find at the theater before the curtain goes up. An orchestra that was part of the evening's "performance," which is what it turned out to be rather than a worship service, began to tune their instruments as orchestras do. The senior minister finally stepped to the stage and welcomed everyone, made a few comical remarks, and said that we were all there to have a great time. That set the tone for everything that followed.

It was a grand production. Everything flowed like clockwork, including the movements of the singers and the raising and lowering of the lights. The narration was dramatic, the singers were gifted, and the music professional. At one point the senior minister gave a short homily. He was smooth and skilled. He fit in perfectly with the others. The service ended with candlelight communion. By the time the whole thing was over I had the uneasy feeling that I had participated in an act of idolatry. Nothing about what was done had any sense of authenticity or genuineness, though the individuals themselves might have been sincere. We didn't worship God. We watched people perform. It all seemed contrived and false. There was no sense of "realness" to it. The members of that church probably "enjoyed" the program, for this is what they apparently get on a regular basis. It has its appeal.

Contrast this experience with a story from the Brooklyn Tabernacle. David Ruffin was a homeless alcoholic who slept on the steps of the Tabernacle. During the day he sold cans to get enough money to buy more wine. At night he could hear the marvelous Brooklyn Tabernacle Choir singing. One Easter Sunday evening David walked through the doors of the Tabernacle and went up the steps to the balcony of the sanctuary. He went in because he decided that this was the Lord's house and he could go in just like he was. Yet he was surprised that no one asked him to leave.

During the service he heard the testimony of a woman who had been a drug addict whose life had been changed by her personal encounter with Jesus Christ. When Pastor Jim Cymbala extended the altar call, David went forward. When Pastor Cymbala saw him standing in the front of the sanctuary, sheepishly looking at him, and smelling worse than any human being he had ever smelled in his life, his first thought was, "Oh, man, what a way to end an Easter Sunday. Someone's going to hit me up for money," something that happened frequently in that neighborhood. But when David stood face-to-face with Pastor Cymbala, he pointed his finger at the minister and said, "Reverend, I don't want your money. I want this Jesus you've been talking about. I'm going to die out there. I don't have a hope in this world if somebody doesn't change me."

At that moment Pastor Cymbala was convicted of his lack of love and compassion. His hands fell to his side and he found himself beginning to weep. He then felt David Ruffin's face fall against his chest and they embraced one another. Later David described that moment saying, "When I fell against him and embraced him I knew that I was embracing something that was real, that this man stood for the Lord. It was that love that drew me." David Ruffin's life was changed that night. He now sings in the great Brooklyn Tabernacle Choir whose music is being heard all over the world. (Story from: "The Brooklyn Tabernacle Choir—Live...He's Been Faithful," Warner Alliance Video, 1994).

What a contrast in stories! From my perspective it is the difference between artificiality and authenticity. One is the by-product of crass marketing to gain the world. The other is rooted in the simplicity of a commitment to be in the world to make a difference in the lives of people who live on the bottom side of life. Ministers who are marketing their churches, whether they realize it or not, have lost their way. They no longer know what it means to be real and genuine. What is most disturbing is that they are becoming the examples for younger ministers who want to succeed in churches struggling to stay alive.

Their message is clear and dangerous. It is that ministry today has to compete with the entertainment culture of our society, even if it means sacrificing being real and genuine, being the real thing, and living out of authentic commitment and concern. The message is that being a minister is playing a role rather than being a role model. The message is that the end justifies the means. It is a message that more and more ministers are preaching and teaching as the pressures grow to do anything to stem the tide of decline.

Despite the fact that some church members get caught up in this kind of leadership, I am convinced most of them see through it. They know that in the long run superficiality in ministry can never serve their needs or meet their deepest spiritual longings. They know that this kind of imitation of the real thing turns out to be as superficial and unsatisfying in the church as it does in the world.

Every minister ought to know it as well. Ministers should in fact be the ones who teach and preach what is real and what is imitation regarding the gospel. Whether ministers believe it or not, their leadership is the most influential factor in the direction and quality of any congregation's ministry. Ministers determine real ministry, and also bear the responsibility for ministry that is a cheap imitation of the real thing.

Ministers Need to Use Common Sense

Not everyone can be brilliant, but everyone can be wise. At least most people can be. It doesn't take knowledge for one to be wise. It takes understanding. Knowledge helps. It doesn't guarantee wisdom. Some common sense does. Common sense produces a fundamental wisdom that leads people to make better decisions and to act and react to circumstances in more constructive ways than they otherwise would.

We have already mentioned the subtle death of common sense that is happening in our society, and the fact that it can happen in the church as well. The problem with ministers is not the death of common sense, that is, the failure to exercise individual judgment. The problem with ministers is the failure to use the common sense they have.

Common sense is essential in ministry. Ministers simply have to have common sense, not just to do effective ministry, but to survive. More ministers get into more trouble than they ever should, because of their failure to use a little common sense. Every minister has common sense, so the problem lies in their not using what they have. There is nothing in ministry that does not require a dose of common sense to make it effective, successful, sensitive, or helpful. Although common sense cannot take the place of basic competence, it can and does enhance or diminish how ministers are perceived by their church members.

A number of church members have mentioned to me enough times some specific ways ministers fail to use common sense that I am convinced these problems are rather commonplace. Let me name some of them.

One is basic personal hygiene. In more instances than I ever thought about, church members have been put in the awkward position of having to talk to their minister about the importance of regular bathing and the use of body deodorant. Others have had to speak to their minister about the need to keep his hands clean, especially when he has to break the communion bread that is to be consumed by the people.

Personal appearance has also been a problem in the ministries of more than a few clergy. A colleague serving in the same small town where I once served had a habit of showing up at meetings barefoot. He felt quite comfortable about it, but many of his members did not. Others have been known to wear shoes during worship services that not only have never been polished, but are caked with mud. More than once student associates have been confronted by church members about the inappropriateness of wearing thongs in the pulpit. One student who had been asked to serve as Sunday worship leader did so wearing a mini-skirt and was shocked at the criticism she received.

All of these things may seem trite and unimportant. On a scale of one to ten in measuring the great issues facing the church, they would no doubt rank very low. But people will not ignore these kinds of problems when they persist. Most church members have a high tolerance level, but issues such as these stretch them beyond their limits. It takes only a little common sense for ministers to avoid this kind of thing.

Sometimes the lack of common sense shows up in a way that reveals a serious lack of reverence on the part of the minister. One example was when a judicatory minister addressed a district gathering of members from several churches. He was standing in front of the communion table, and at one point during his conversation with them he sat on top of it. They never heard another word he said, not to mention the lingering problems his actions created regarding his credibility with them.

The list of offenses could go on. The point is simply that ministry is one area of service where common sense is essential. Its absence can sometimes cause irreparable damage to a ministry. Church members have a right to expect their minister to use common sense. To suggest that decorum and social grace are important is not bending to false values. It is, rather, to acknowledge the reality that church members do not abandon proper manners and behavior when they go to church. It is true that "what" is done is more important than "how," but only the very foolish dismiss "how" as unimportant. Ministers build credibility several ways. One of them is in the use of common sense. No minister should forget this simple but important fact.

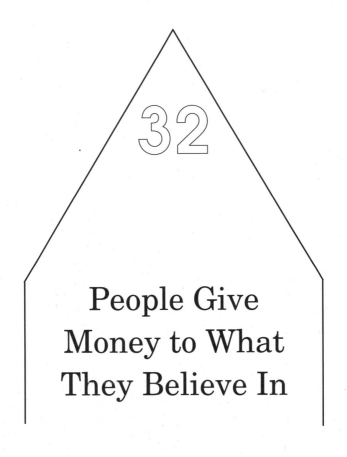

People Give
Money to What
They Believe In

Financial support for the church is one dimension of Christian stewardship. Ministers generally challenge church members to give as an expression of taking their stewardship responsibilities seriously. This means to give with no strings attached, especially the string of designating to specific causes members might want their money to go to. Basically ministers want church members to give to the church unconditionally.

Theologically there are good grounds for this approach to financial stewardship. A Christian's money, like time, talents, attitudes, and actions, should be based upon love for God, not upon agreement or disagreement with what the church is doing or not doing. After all, what church has all its members agreeing all the time with all it does?

132

It is an impossible expectation. If financial support to congregations and denominations depended entirely upon people's agreeing with everything they do, most would not survive for long.

At the same time, though, church members wish ministers would face up to the practical reality that most people, church members included, support the things they believe in, and refuse to support what they don't believe in. In general people exercise this right when it comes to nonchurch types of solicitations. A colleague, for example, has a standing policy regarding telephone solicitations. He tells the caller that he never gives a donation over the phone, but is willing to examine literature the organization can send and then make a decision. This is the only way he will consider making a donation.

This is a responsible way to make such decisions. Good stewardship includes making good decisions about what to support. It is not responsible stewardship to hand out donations indiscriminately, and not solely because of the fraudulent appeals for money that seem to abound today. Good stewardship also involves learning about the people and their ministries and causes before support is given. A position to which I have arrived only of late is that this is as true for the church as any other group or organization. The notion that people give to what they believe in is not only a fact of life that ministers need to face, but it can be a mark of good stewardship.

The day of gracious loyalty to the church has come to an end. Ministers can no longer take for granted that people will financially support their church out of loyalty. Church members want to know where their money is going and how it is being spent. They are not willing to give to the church unconditionally, especially when the church sometimes uses money for causes church members do not want to support.

This kind of discriminating financial support on the part of church members first began to assert itself on the denominational level. For years my own denomination used a system of giving that assumed churches trusted giving to a unified denominational budget that was sliced into percentages for the various agencies of our church. That worked until people began to disagree with some of the ways the agencies were spending money, exacerbated by a growing disenchantment with the leaders of those agencies. After years of feeling like their concerns were being ignored, churches began to express their dissatisfaction by limiting their giving or stopping it altogether. One result has been that local churches have finally gotten the attention of denominational leaders.

This kind of discriminating approach to financial support is now showing up on the local level. People are less willing than they used to be to give to their church without knowing how the money will be spent or to give when their money is supporting things they don't agree with. They want to believe in the ministries they are being asked to support. They are less willing even on the local level to leave decisions about how money is spent to a few people. This is especially true in congregations where some members believe their minister holds views that are much more liberal than their own.

Ministers can lament this new situation, or they can see it as an opportunity to do what they should have been doing (some have) all along—educating their members about the ministries the minister wants them to support. The fact that people give to what they believe in, and seldom give—or give much—to what they don't believe in or know much about, may be what at our seminary we call "a teaching moment" in the church. The more information people have about what they are being asked to support financially, the stronger their support is likely to be. This offers ministers an opportunity to do some serious stewardship education regarding the specific ways their churches are trying to live the gospel.

This is also a situation that is calling ministers to give an account for their own leadership, and to recognize the relationship between financial support and something previously discussed—ministers running too far ahead of their members. (See chapter 18.) This is not to suggest that ministers need to see which way the wind is blowing in their church, and not to sail against it. That would be a loss of integrity, a price too high to pay. It is, instead, a candid recognition that when church members give to those things they believe in they are saying that the church's leadership, i.e., ministers, needs to stay in touch with where they are, and to take their concerns about ministry seriously. It is not a matter of agreement or disagreement about a particular ministry. It is a matter of leadership. Ministers who are out of touch with church members are not likely to persuade them to support the church. This is one thing ministers *can* take to the bank!

It is human nature to give to what one believes in, and not give to things one does not believe in. The gospel changes persons, but so far as we can tell it does not alter human nature itself—which means church members will continue to have this attitude about financial stewardship. It is up to ministers to give the kind of leadership that taps their generosity.

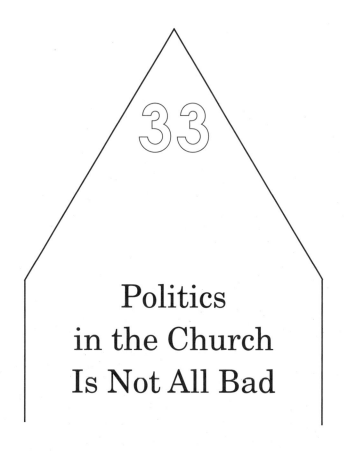

Politics
in the Church
Is Not All Bad

As a rule ministers don't like church politics. As another rule, ministers are responsible for most of the politics in the church, and know how to play the game quite well. As a third rule, politics will always be part of church life. This is because the church is made up of people, which means *power* is a broker in the church. Decisions in the church, as in all institutions, are affected by the use of power among those in leadership.

Nobody likes politics when decisions go against them. When decisions go their way they don't think about them as being a result of the political use of power. But that's what it is most of the time. In a perfect world people would make decisions based upon love and justice. We don't live in a perfect world, so decisions are based upon love, justice—and power! In order to get anything accomplished in the church, politics becomes an avenue of reality. Moreover, it is more than a little disingenuous for anyone in the church, especially ministers, to cry foul when they see politics at work. Human beings are political animals precisely because we want to get things done. Getting things done involves soliciting the support of others. That is the game of politics. It is difficult to imagine how any minister can effectively lead a church without using political power.

The definition of the word *politic* suggests following a direction based upon a definite "policy." In other words, to be political means to believe in a certain "policy" that guides one's actions on behalf of the success of that policy. In other words, politics is the right use of power. The late Martin Luther King, Jr., in his book *Where Do We Go from Here?* (Harper & Row, 1977), defined power in a way all ministers should ponder. He wrote that "power, properly understood, is the ability to achieve purpose....In this sense power is not only desirable, but necessary in order to implement the demands of love and justice" (p. 37). He went on to show the flaw of thinking that love and power are polar opposites. "Power," he said, "at its best is love implementing the demands of justice. Justice at its best is love correcting everything that stands against love" (p. 37).

Politics in the church, when the nature of power is properly understood, is the right use of power at work to accomplish a good goal or purpose. The right use of power becomes the means by which that which is "right" gets accomplished. Ministers are people who try to accomplish what they believe is the right thing. The use of power is a necessary tool in ministry. It is morally right for ministers to be political. For at its best being political means using power on behalf of what one believes is a good thing. Nothing is wrong with this kind of leadership in ministry. It simply calls on ministers to be careful to examine just what it is they are trying to do to see whether they are working on behalf of gospel values.

The late President Lyndon Johnson used to say that politics is the art of the possible. Ministers need to think about this before they decry politics in the church. Learning the art of the possible means learning how to give and take on issues, learning how to win and lose, learning how to accept gracefully not always getting one's way. Jesus told us that with God all things are possible (Matthew 19:26). He was referring to the specific question of salvation for people like the rich young ruler who had turned away from Jesus rather than giving up his wealth, but the church has appropriately taught that this statement has general application in calling Christians not to limit what they seek to do to what appears possible. Yet it is often the right use of power, i.e., being political, that enables Christians to move mountains once thought immovable.

It is not only naive for ministers to pretend they can stay above church politics in providing leadership; it is hypocritical. Playing the game of church politics does not mean a minister is dishonest or self-serving. It means the minister is facing the realities of how to work with people to accomplish important goals.

Ministers who don't like church politics are probably ministers who either don't know how to lead people to action or who haven't gotten their way on an issue.

Is this an issue church members really want their minister to know about? After all, don't many church members join ministers in criticizing politics in the church? The answer to both questions is *yes*. Church members sometimes are frustrated and even angry about church politics, but it is usually for the same reasons ministers are—naïveté about human nature and not getting their way. At the same time church members also want their minister to get things done. They don't want their church treading water. Thus, consciously or unconsciously they want strong and decisive leadership that points the direction the church needs to follow. Ministers who do this will not always have initial support for what they want to do. That is where politics comes in to help win support.

Church members want a minister who knows how to work within the realities of congregational life. They may call it by a different name, but it is no more than learning the art of the possible. It is the game of politics, and it's not all bad!

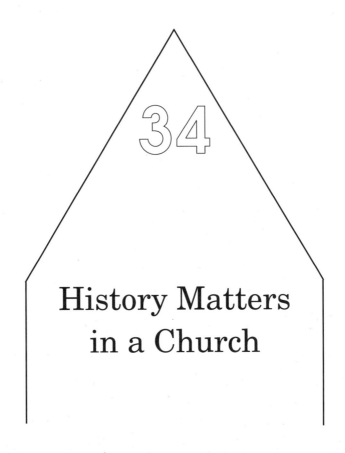

History Matters
in a Church

Telling stories is one of my family's favorite pastimes when we all get together. We tell stories on ourselves and on one another, on our dogs and cats, on our friends and others, on whoever and whatever comes to mind. Most families do this. It is a way of staying in touch with our past. More than that, it is a way of keeping alive through memory those people we have loved and who have loved us. It is a way of identifying the moments that have shaped our lives and in some measure have made us into the people we have become.

In the last several years story has become a widely used method of reading and interpreting the Bible. Scholars try to help readers understand God and God's relationship to the world via the stories the Bible tells. Jesus made use of stories when he talked about the rule of God on earth and in heaven. Seeing the stories of scripture enables us to appreciate and even experience the rich heritage and tradition that are ours as Christians. In these stories we often find our own identity as contemporary members of the covenant people of God.

One of my doctoral students is designing a project to assist church members in making connections with scripture stories through the telling and retelling of their own faith stories. Her thesis is that in telling their stories people begin to understand as never before the hand of God at work in their lives. In this way faith moves from things believed to experiences that shape and guide what one believes. In an amazing way stories tell us who we are in a refreshing way, in a way that even surprises us sometimes. Not to know our own story is in a very real sense not to know who we are.

What is true for individuals is also true for churches. Every church has a story to tell that describes the persons and events that have shaped and at the same time revealed its identity. In every congregation there are members who know their church's story and love to tell it. Their story is a piece of the oral tradition of both Israel and the church that has played an essential role among the people of God from one generation to another in providing direction and hope. The last thing a church needs is amnesia, that state of forgetfulness wherein the traditions and persons and events of the past are lost in time. Amnesia is an enemy of churches. It robs them of roots that give strength and nourishment to ministry.

Unfortunately there are too many ministers who want their churches to have amnesia. They are tired of hearing about the ways things used to be, and especially about the way past ministers used to do things. They view stories of the past as an unnecessary encumbrances to present and future progress. These ministers cringe when they hear church members talking about the past. What they don't seem to realize is that these people are talking about their identity as a church. Some of them may want to live in the past, but most of them simply do not want to forget where they have been. They may be frightened about an uncertain future, but they have sense enough to know they cannot resuscitate what used to be. They just don't want to be cut off from it because they don't want to lose their identity in a world that changes daily.

More than anything else, ministers need to understand that history is as important to a church as it is to an individual. Story provides a solid foundation for the future. Ministers who spend time educating their people about their church's past are the ones who generally find them more open to change. Nothing builds resistance to change faster in the church than a minister who acts as if nothing important happened before he came to the church. It is the minister who knows and appreciates a congregation's history who can invite her church members to pay tribute to those who have gone before by rising to the challenges of a new day. That is, after all, what those in the past did in order to prepare for the way to the future now being lived. When church members know this they understand why they must do the same.

In the book *Good News in Growing Churches* (United Church Press, 1990), editor Robert L. Burt brings together stories of congregations that have made strides toward renewed life and vigor. A critical reading of these stories raises questions about how "good" the news really is in these churches. But what is instructive in the book are stories about several historic churches that experienced renewed life under the leadership of ministers who drew upon the rich heritage and tradition of their congregations to make a doorway into the future. These ministers found their church members more than willing to respond to change when they also connected the future toward which they were moving with the traditions that meant so much to them.

This is the kind of wise and sensible leadership churches today need. The heritage and traditions of many congregations form an untapped resource for progress if ministers would only take advantage of them. They are also a guide to avoiding pitfalls that have caused ministers in the past to stumble. History is a great teacher only when the student pays attention to it. At the very least it is more than a little shortsighted to think that appreciating the past means one is resistant to new ideas or unwilling to confront the realities of the present age. Every congregation has a story to tell. Ministers ought to know that story and then make sure their church members learn it and learn how to tell it well. The gospel does not exist in a vacuum, but in the lives of ordinary people whose story of trying to live it can be a source of inspiration and courage for anyone who takes the time to learn about it. Ministers of all people should understand how true this is.

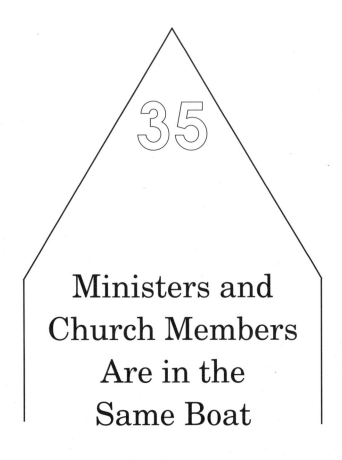

Ministers and Church Members Are in the Same Boat

In *What Ministers Wish...*, and now in this volume, a simple theme has undergirded everything that has been said. It is the theme of shared responsibility among clergy and laity for the health and well-being of the church. This responsibility is lived out in many ways, perhaps the most important one being the many encounters between ministers and church members that occur daily. Most of the time these encounters seem rather ordinary and even mundane, certainly routine. They are seldom dramatic. But this lack of drama can be deceiving, lulling both ministers and church members into a deadly complacency about the significance of what is happening between them. The importance of these encounters lies

144

more in their cumulative effect over time than in the power of a single moment. A reliable barometer of the extent to which ministers and church members are willing to put the health and well-being of the church above individual interests is the way they work together on a daily basis.

Living as we do at a time when churches are having to scratch and fight just to keep their heads above water, it is disturbing to see ministers and church members so often working at cross-purposes. In more than a few instances they are in outright conflict that ends up dividing the church they claim to care about. An awareness that Christians are being pressed by secularism and de-churched spirituality to unite in common objectives seems to be lost on so many ministers and church members. Whatever else is going on with the church, that Christianity is in transition regarding its status and role in American society—and in the world—is a bit of hard reality every church member and minister can ill afford to take lightly.

What is needed today is a general recognition among ministers and church members that whatever is happening in the church and the world at large must be faced together. Churches no longer have the luxury of infighting. Only the very foolish do not see that the church's witness in today's world requires a unity of spirit that transcends the factions that have divided church in the past. Yet the foolish seem to be winning the day in the church, what with the public rancor and division among Christians so common in all denominations. A distinctive factor that makes the church's witness even weaker is the exploitation of divisions among Christian groups by ideologues on the right and left. Right-wingers use Christianity to advance self-serving agendas. Left-wingers want to expunge anything even remotely religious from public life. Neither serves the best interests of the nation, and certainly not the church. Yet ministers and church members seem more than willing to open themselves to being exploited by their attitude toward one another.

The Bible makes clear that the work of God in the world is not wholly dependent upon the church. Moreover, Christian history is replete with examples of God at work *in spite of* the church. Yet the church remains the body of Christ, and at times acts in amazing ways that witnesses to this reality. As bad as the church is, there is still much ministry it can do. Whatever the future shape of the church turns out to be, if ministry is to be done it will hinge on the awareness that what remains constant from generation to generation is the need for ministers and church members to love and work with one another. This means both must have a burning desire to be the body of Christ before anything else. Both must hunger and thirst after putting the common good before themselves. Both must choose to listen more and talk less, to seek reconciliation rather than control, and to believe that strength is to be found in unity of purpose and spirit more than in numbers.

Ministers and church members wish the other knew more than they do about each other, about ministry, about how to be together in the church. The truth about us all, though, is that none of us will ever live as much as we know or know as much as we ought to. The most we can hope for is understanding and forgiveness in our dealings with each other. The leadership of ministers and church members differs according to the demands of the gospel and the needs of the church and the world. At the same time each is indispensable to the effectiveness of the other. We are in the same boat. We move ahead or float around without direction according to the level of our commitment to working together on behalf of the gospel of Jesus Christ. We need to work hard at being with each other in love and respect because together we need to witness to Jesus in a world full of sorrow. The latter ought to be enough for us to be diligent about the former. It is a sobering thought that someday he will tell us how well we have done at both. Whatever is wrong with the church is the responsibility of ministers and church members alike. Whatever is right with the church is something about which both can rejoice and be glad. Being the body of Christ means at least that the triumphs and failures in every church belong to us all. No one person is to blame. No one person can take the credit. The body is strong or weak as a body. That is the nature of it. Maybe that is why Jesus formed us in this way. We shall rise together or fall together, but either way it will be together. Perhaps that is what Jesus wishes all of us knew.

Phillipa Berta

Offenburg